Deadly Innocent

He may not be guilty of murder,
but his love proved deadly to more than one.

By
Magdel and Paul Roets

PO Box 221974 Anchorage, Alaska 99522-1974
books@publicationconsultants.com
www.publicationconsultants.com

ISBN Number: 978-1-59433-841-0
eBook ISBN Number: 978-1-59433-842-7

Library of Congress Number 2018966718

Copyright 2018 Magdel and Paul Roets
—First Edition—

All rights reserved, including the right of
reproduction in any form, or by any mechanical
or electronic means including photocopying or
recording, or by any information storage or
retrieval system, in whole or in part in any
form, and in any case not without the
written permission of the author and publisher.

Manufactured in the United States of America

Table of Contents

CHAPTER 1	Thorns	5
CHAPTER 2	The Accused	18
CHAPTER 3	The prisoner	30
CHAPTER 4	A New Life	43
CHAPTER 5	Parole	53
CHAPTER 6	Love Rekindled	57
CHAPTER 7	A Free Man	64
CHAPTER 8	The Wedding	77
CHAPTER 9	Another Murder	85

Deadly Innocent

CHAPTER 1

Thorns

She bent over to smell a red bloom, savouring the aroma. Ahh, slowly exhaling, her favorite rose bush, the Mister Langley. She did not hear his approach, the lawn silencing the sound of his footsteps The sweet aroma filled her nose; next her face was in the thorns, her head pushed down by a big, cruel hand. Penelope screamed with pain as she tried to move away from under the hand. This only resulted in more pain as the thorns of the rose bush pierced her skin.

"I've told you before not to walk around in the garden in your sweat suit. Can't you get dressed like any decent human being before you leave your bedroom?"

"It's the gardener's day off. You told me not to walk outside in my sweat suit where the gardener can see me," replies Penelope, avoiding eye contact so he won't see the hatred in her eyes.

"I cancelled his day off. I'm sure he's lurking out there somewhere. I've seen how he looks at you. Now go inside and wash your face. I'll be waiting for you in the sunroom."

Yes, he looks at me in pity, she thought while cleaning the blood from her face. She wondered what the poor old man thought every time he had to observe an encounter like this. Carefully she applied make-up to conceal the marks the thorns left on her skin. Not to agitate the man further, she chose an outfit her husband liked, dressed quickly, pulled a brush through her thick, dark-brown hair and looked at her image in the mirror. Beauty restored, composure intact, she walked down the stairs.

Entering the sunroom, she paused for a moment to allow him to assess her appearance, then walked proudly, stately towards the sitting area where she fluttered down into her favorite easy chair, waiting for his usual apologies. It was all an act. They both acted civilized, well-bred and they both knew it was nothing but a farce. A well-rehearsed act on a self-created stage. Their own private stage where they could fool themselves by pretending they fool each other.

Brendon reached into his jacket, pulled out his wallet and took out one of many credit cards. Remorse all over his face, he handed her the card.

"Take this and go out today. I want you to treat yourself on something special. Go to a spa, go shopping, go to see a show, whatever you feel like doing. Go and enjoy yourself." She took the card from his hand, but he grabbed her hand, pulled it closer and kissed it gently.

"Penny, I'm sorry. I don't know what came over me. I didn't mean to hurt you. Please, forgive me." She kept her facial expression neutral not to reveal her true feelings.

"Of course. What are your plans for today?"

"That's what I wanted to talk to you about. I have to be in Chicago this afternoon. I'll be leaving in an hour."

"Do you want me to pack for you?"

"No, thanks. The maid already has. Everything's ready."

"How long will you be away?"

"If all goes according to plan I should be back by Friday. Look, I'm sorry to leave you alone at home so soon after the previous trip. This is not a scheduled one. Things just happened and now the shareholders want answers. But when I get back I want you and me, just the two of us, to go somewhere quiet. Would you like that?"

"Sure," she said with a faint smile. "Perhaps that is just what we need."

* * * *

What she needed was the safety of her living quarters at home. The weekend in the woods did not go well. Brendon was agitated at every little detail that was not to his taste. The wood for the fire-place was not dry enough, causing it to smoke. The cottage was damp. The fragrant candles gave him headache. The food was not right. However hard she tried to please him, nothing was satisfying.

* * * *

Penelope turned round in front of the wall to wall, floor to ceiling mirror in her dressing-room. She looked well, she had to admit. The full-length, one shoulder, black dress still fitted well, although a bit on the loose side. She must have lost a pound or two. This dress was her favorite; simple, elegant, with just a touch of bling on the curvy embroidery, enhanced by a few Swarovski crystals, emphasizing the diagonal neckline. The dress flared out subtly from the knees down to the ankles to show off an elegant pair of three-inch stiletto shoes. The only jewelry she wore, was a pair of diamond-in-platinum earrings; a birthday gift from her loving husband, and a Rolex on her left arm. She would try not to move the arm too much, the weight of the Rolex caused a bit of discomfort.

The bruises on her neck and left shoulder had faded, the cast was taken off her left arm, and the tiny scar above her left eyebrow was made invisible by make-up. Little evidence of the violence by the cottage in the woods, was left on her body. For the scars in her soul, there was no healing.

The memory of her first visit Brendon grabbing her by the neck and slamming her full force into the pine tree in front of the cottage was still vivid in her mind. They were walking down-hill towards the cottage. She managed a reflex half twist that time, saving her face. Oh she loved him then and forgave. Now too many years of tiptoeing through this marriage and abuse, had made her determined to end it. She planned it. Soon, she will be free.

"Now this is life," Brendon said in a good mood after a brisk, early-morning walk in the woods surrounding their weekend cottage.

"Fresh air, birdsong and the prettiest lady by my side. We should do it more often."

"Sure, sell everything and let us move here permanently."

"I wish it were that simple."

"It is that simple. We don't need New York."

"My business is in New York. I can't sell it. Not now."

"You can run your business from here. Internet reception is not too bad. All you need is your computer."

"And what will I do to keep busy? Twiddle my fingers?" By now his mood was changing for the worse. She realized, too late, that she had better change the subject.

"We can sit in front of the fireplace twiddling our fingers together," she said playfully.

"Or maybe I should move here and you can join me over weekends." That was when it happened. Yelling: "You will never leave me," he grabbed her by the arm. She tried to pull free, but he grabbed her hair, pulling her closer. The fear in her eyes made the anger in him explode. He grabbed her by the neck and with all his might, threw her against the tree five feet away from them. It happened so fast, there was nothing she could do to avoid the tree. She flew like a ragdoll and smashed into it with a sickening thud. Pain shot through her arm and shoulder. Her head was spinning. Dazed and hurting she fell to the ground while he stood there watching.

At the emergency room he told the doctor she slipped on loose stones and fell. Another lie, to another Physician. Whether he was believed, no one will know. Her arm was put in a cast and she was sent home with two dozen pain tablets. In the car on their way back to the cottage Brendon tried to break through the silence with silly remarks like: "The leaves will soon be falling," and "look, there are squirrels in those trees". He gave up when she responded with a grunt or a single-word answer.

"I should have picked up something to eat while we were still in town."

"It's OK. I'm sure I can put something together."

"With your arm in a cast? Won't it be too painful?" She shot him a brief look that says 'whose fault is that?', but shrugged and said: "What if I tell you exactly what to do and you do the work?" With guilt feelings plaguing him, he just might fall for it. They both knew he could not boil water without a recipe. And so he did; prepare a meal that was half decent, under strict guidance and supervision.

That was five weeks ago, and here she stood in front of her mirror, trying to work up the courage to face all the people downstairs. Her first public appearance after her "accident" in the woods. A birthday party in her honor, with all their friends, Brendon's brother and a few business partners. Twenty-eight years old and a wreck by the hand of an abusive husband. A woman who will never be a mother because of the damage done to her insides during the early second-trimester of her first and only pregnancy two years ago. She turned away from the mirror and started walking out on the landing towards the stairs. The guests were waiting.

* * * *

Simon approached Penelope the moment she was not crowded by people.

"Happy birthday, Penelope," he placed a tender kiss on her cheek and a small parcel in her hand.

"Thank you so much." She smiled at her brother-in-law. He is the total opposite from Brendon. He is kind and gentle and a family man. Tilda spotted them across the room and waddled forth in their direction.

"Congrats, Penny, and many happy returns. I'm so glad my husband finally got a chance with you. The people have been circling you, it's hard to get to you." Touching her big, round belly, she smiled and said: "Especially for one my size. I see Simon gave you our gift." For some strange reason, Penelope felt a little disappointed to learn the gift was from both of them, which meant Tilda probably chose it. But the feeling disappeared when Tilda continued: "He was the one who chose it for you. Hope you like it. I just don't want to go shopping any more than I have to, you know."

"Of course not. Thank you for the gift. I'm sure Simon chose well. How long to go?"

"Three weeks. Thank goodness. And then the sleepless nights again. Gaby is just beginning to sleep through the night, and now the next one is not even born yet and already kicking me awake at night.

"You know, Tilda you are so lucky. You are the best mother I know. Your kids are happy to have you as their mom. Both of you. You are the best parents ever."

"And I am the luckiest husband," said Brendon behind her, joining them. "Good to have you, brother. Tilda, glad you could still make it."

"I wouldn't miss my favorite sis-in-law's birthday unless I was in labor." They all laughed heartily, some people joining them. One of the men, Greg Atwood, asked Simon: "So, Simon, what's new in the firearm business." The men immediately started talking guns and ammunition, separating themselves from the women, who started talking babies and birth matters.

* * * *

Greg and his girlfriend, Sandy, watched the crowd.

"Are you ready for tonight?"

"Are you sure the time is right?"

"Sure, Baby. It's the perfect time to do the job." He touched her nose with a finger: "We planned this well and we're going through with it. We're not backing down now."

"If you say so, handsome." Sandy smiled, showing a row of perfect white teeth.

Penelope, being the lady of the evening, excused herself from the group to circulate again. The patio doors were open and a pleasant breeze blew in. It was a lovely late summer evening. In a few weeks it will be too chilly to be outside at night. The guests realize that, and made the most of it, dancing or sitting out on the dimly lit patio. The moon was almost full and for the younger couples it was a very romantic setting. Soft music, moonlight and the breeze carrying fragrances from the flowers in the garden. She stepped outside with a glass of champagne, knowing Brendon would follow her, as his eyes never left her for a moment.

"Shall we dance?" he took her glass, put it down and took her in his arms. "You are by far the most beautiful woman here. I love you so much."

"Then why do you always hurt me?"

"I don't know. But let's not talk about it tonight. Let's just enjoy the romance of the evening. I promise you I'll make an appointment with a councilor tomorrow." He drew her close to him, swaying gently to the music.

"May I cut in? I haven't had time to congratulate the lady yet." Brendon let go of her reluctantly. As he turned, he saw, or thought he saw a shadow among the shrubs at the edge of the garden. He looked again, but it was gone. Probably his imagination, but he will let his maintenance man have a look at the motion detectors in the morning. When he turned back to watch his wife dancing with Greg, he noticed the man was holding her much tighter than what could be considered appropriate.

"That's enough. I want my wife back."

"Hey, man, what's the matter? I just got her."

"Back off, Greg, she's my wife and I want her back." Greg stood aside with a sarcastic bow as if Brendon was a king and "accidentally" gave Brendon's arm a shove in the process.

"Don't do that, Greg, I'm warning you."

"It's alright, Brendon, he meant no harm. Probably had one too many. Let's not make a scene. The people are already staring. Let's dance." Penelope stepped in front of him in a dancing movement, took his hand and turned him away from Greg. He put his arm possessively around her slender waist and danced away.

* * * *

Later Brendon stood at the bar chatting to some friends when a man approached him.

"What do you want, Williams? I don't recall inviting you?" Continuing in a scarcely audible voice, he said: "the friggen partners are here, I told you we should not be seen together and here you turn up at my house during a party."

"Just a word in private, please, then I'll go." They moved away from the crowd, to talk outside on the patio, in a quiet corner close to the garden.

"About the take-over ..."

* * * *

Greg checked his watch. He should have delayed Brendon longer. Penelope should not have intervened. But at least she kept him busy for a while. He turned to go inside to look for his woman and almost knocked her over.

"I was just going to look for you. Did you do it?" Smiling ever so sweetly she patted her little handbag: "Of course I did. Nothing to worry about now."

"Did anyone see you?"

"How do you know me? Am I the best burglar or am I the best burglar? That safe was like a locker in a high school. And there was nobody. When are you going to confront him?"

"Maybe soon. Williams is already here."

"Williams will aggravate him, and, and, and ...."

"And we will be long gone. All fingers will point to Williams."

"You are such a genius. How did you know Williams will be here?"

"There is little I don't know. I can sniff out secret meetings from a distance. You sure no one saw you?"

"Sure I'm sure. Besides, I have an alibi."

"Who?"

"The lady of the house herself. I went to the ladies-room afterward and she was there. She looked a bit flustered but when I asked, she said she was OK."

"I wonder what that was all about. Perhaps Brendon gave her a hard time for letting me hold her."

"You did what?"

"I held her tight to make him jealous."

"Well now, you probably enjoyed it. Couldn't you think of something else to keep him occupied?"

"I didn't enjoy it half as much as holding you, Sweetheart." He put his arm around her and squeezed her tightly, thinking 'no more blackmailing me, now that there is nothing incriminating against me I can go after the man himself. Our company will swallow his. Williams will see to that'.

* * * *

The party was in full swing and everybody was having fun. No one noticed the absence of another. The house was big and people moved around. If anyone was not at a certain point at any given time, no one would notice. Even if the host or hostess disappeared for a few minutes, no one would find it strange.

"Have you seen Brendon?" Tilda asked a friend passing by.

"He was at the bar a while ago with my husband. Maybe they're still around there."

"Thanks, Dianne. Perhaps Simon is also there." Tilda walked heavily towards the bar to find her husband and their host. She wanted to thank their host, collect her husband and go home. She had already told Penelope, repeated her good wishes and thanked her for a lovely evening. Being short and not wearing high heels, Tilda had to stretch and weave among the people to see who is at the bar. Simon was just moving away towards the patio with Dianne's husband, Andy and someone she didn't know. Quickly she changed course to intercept Simon and tell him it's time to leave.

"Simon, Honey, I'm really tired. Would you mind very much if we go?"

"Of course not. Let's find Brendon and Penny and then we'll be off."

"I already said good bye to Penny for both of us. She understands. But I thought Brendon was with you."

"We were together at the bar, but some guy I don't know, came and talked to him. They excused themselves and left. Andy, do you know the man who spoke to Brendon?"

"I've seen him before, but I don't know him. Could be one of Brendon's managers."

"Manager? Would Brendon invite a manager to a party?"

"I know it sounds strange, but he is definitely not a partner."

"Yea, I know all the partners. Ah, well, they know lots of people. You can't know everyone. I just wonder why Brendon looked so upset."

"I noticed it too. It's supposed to be a party, not a business meeting."

"Yea, well, you know Brendon. I bet he takes his laptop with him to church."

"If he ever takes the time to go."

"Sorry to interrupt, guys, but I really need to go. See you, Andy. C'mon, Sweetheart, let's be off."

* * * *

The party was fizzing out. A few late-nighters were still hanging onto their drinks, but most guests were ready to leave.

"Where's Brendon? We'd like to say good night," asked Henry.

"He should be with Penelope. There she is. Brendon should be close by."

"I don't see him anywhere."

"Penelope, thanks for a great evening. Your parties are always the best."

"Henry, Susan, thanks for coming. Great to have you, always."

"I don't see Brendon anywhere. Will you tell him we said good-bye?"

"He's probably out on the patio seeing guests off. But if you don't find him, I'll tell him you came to say good-bye."

"Henry, she actually looks pale to me. Quite exhausted really. Good thing the party is over," Susan said as soon as Penelope was no longer within hearing distance.

"Exhausted? She looks bewildered to me."

"Penelope, it's been a nice party. And you look radiant as always. Not a day older, just ... better."

"Thanks so much for coming. Good night." And so it went for a few more minutes until a scream filled the air. A commotion followed.

"Call an ambulance!" someone shouted.

"Call the police," another ordered.

"Who's gonna tell Penelope?"

"Tell me what?" Penelope asked wide eyed, trying to get through to the garden where the shouting was coming from. Someone grabbed her by the arm:

"No, you're not going there. Come, sit down. Bring me a glass of water, anyone!" David Tanner shouted.

"For goodness sake, what is going on? David, talk to me." David handed her a glass of water.

"Here, drink."

"I'm not thirsty, I'm curious. What is going on?"

"It's Brendon"

"What about Brendon? Where is he? Everybody has been looking for him?"

"He ... sorry, Penelope, he is in the garden."

"What is unusual about that? Sorry about what? Has something happened to him?" Penelope now started to look worried. The glass in her hand was no longer steady.

"He is lying among the roses. It looks like he is hurt, or something." She tried to get up to go out, but David stopped her.

"No, don't go. The ambulance will be here soon." Again she tried to get up, but David held her down, his hand on her shoulder. With quivering hand, she took a sip of water.

CHAPTER 2

The Accused

To David it seemed like hours, but in fact, it was only minutes later that the paramedics arrived with a police patrol car right behind. The paramedics rushed to the rose garden where they were directed to by some bystanders. One look at Brendon and they retreated. After a brief exchange between the ambulance driver and the patrolman, the paramedics left. Having received a major emergency call from dispatch about a pile-up on the highway, and with obviously nothing they could do here, they left the scene for the police to do their investigation. The patrolman asked everybody to retreat to the party lounge and radioed for homicide, who had already sent out a team directly after the 911 call came in. They did not wait long for the homicide detectives to arrive.

It did not take long for the detectives to come up with a suspect. Penelope, already pale, looked as if all blood drained from her face when the detective entered the house telling her they have arrested Floyd Davies, the gardener. They found him sneaking around near the rose garden where the body was found. They also found a nine millimeter, that they considered to be the murder weapon. Forensic tests will reveal the truth, they believed.

* * * *

"Mister Crawford, tell the court about the night Brendon Shaw was murdered."

"I went out onto the patio for a bit of fresh air. The party was breaking up and there were no one on the patio when I saw a movement among the shrubs. I was a bit apprehensive, but I took the courage to go closer to see what it was. As I went around one of the rosebushes, I stumbled over something. It was one of Brendon Shaw's legs. He was lying on his back in an awkward position in a rosebush. There was a large, dark patch in the middle of his chest. At first I thought it was mud, but calling his name, he did not react. I realized then it was not mud, couldn't have been. I figured what might have happened and called 911 straight away."

"No questions from the defense, your Honor."

"Next witness. Call Dianne Crawford." As soon as she was sworn in, Dianne was asked to give her account of the events of that night.

"Your Honor, I was saying goodbye to some friends who were leaving the party when I realized my husband was not in the room. It was late and I thought we should be going too. Everybody was looking for Mr. Shaw, to say good-bye, but no one had seen him for a while. So, I started looking for Andy, my husband. I found him outside talking on his cell phone and found it odd that he would be phoning anyone that late. I went closer and saw Brendon, Mr. Shaw lying in the bush. I couldn't help but scream. People came out and started shouting. David Tanner was there and when he saw Brendon, Mr. Shaw, he went straight inside to talk to Penelope. Shortly after that the police arrived."

"No further questions." The next witness was David Tanner.

"I was looking for Mr. Shaw to say good night. I saw him earlier going out onto the patio with Mr. Williams, and since no one had seen him after that, I assumed I'd find him there, when I heard screaming from outside. When I reached the place in the garden where I saw Mr. and Mrs. Crawford standing, I went closer to see what the matter was. Brendon Shaw was lying on his back in a rosebush. I realized he must have been seriously hurt, or dead. While Andy Crawford had already called 911, I went back in to talk to Mrs. Shaw. I was not sure how to break the news. I certainly didn't want to tell her he was dead, because he might still be alive, however remote the possibility. She wanted to go out to him, but I stopped her. She looked tired and fragile, so I thought it best to keep her as calm as possible and break the news gently, gradually."

"Mr. Atwood, Greg Atwood, tell us about your experiences on the night of the murder."

"As I left early, I don't have much to tell. We, my girlfriend and I enjoyed the party, I danced with Mrs. Shaw, congratulated her on her birthday and soon after that, we went home."

"Why did you leave so early?"

"Sandy, my girlfriend complained of headache, so we went home."

"Did you say good night to your hosts?"

"Yes, of course. We had to explain why we were leaving such a lovely party so early."

"So, Mr. Shaw was available? You saw him and spoke to him?"

"Naturally. He was speaking to someone I didn't know, but we cut in, said bye and left."

"Did Mr. Shaw seem normal, friendly?"

"He looked a bit upset, but I didn't take it to heart. Maybe the guy he was talking to, said something he didn't like."

"You didn't do anything to upset him?"

"Absolutely not. We were close friends. I danced with his wife, he cut in, like a jealous husband, but all in good humor."

"No further questions from the prosecution."

"Does the defense have any questions for this witness?"

"Not right now, your Honor, but the defense require for this witness to be available until the trial is over."

"Mr. Williams," the defense attorney said to the next witness, "you were the last person who saw the deceased alive. What were you doing at the party on the night of the murder? I believe you were not invited?"

"Your honor, I had some urgent business to discuss with Mr. Shaw."

"Why didn't you call him on the phone? Why crash the party?"

"I just popped in for a moment to give him a message and schedule a meeting. As I was in the vicinity and the matter too delicate to discuss on the phone, I thought it best to drop in quickly, say what I had to say and leave. He was alive when I left."

"He was alive, but strangely, no one saw him alive after that. Shortly after you left him, he was found dead in a rosebush. No more questions."

This ended the first day of the trial of the State against Floyd Davies.

* * * *

The next day Simon Shaw was called to the stand. Again the prosecution asked some standard questions before the defense took over.

"Mister Shaw, please tell the court your version of the events on the night of the murder of Brendon Shaw. He was your brother, right?"

"Yes, he was."

"My condolences, Sir."

"Thank you."

"Please, proceed."

"It was a party like any other, I suppose. Everyone was in a good mood. My wife was highly pregnant at the time. She got tired and wanted to leave early. She told me she had already said good night to my sister-in-law, Penelope. Someone said Brendon went aside to speak to a person unknown to us and we didn't know exactly where he was. Not to waste time we just left, assuming he would understand. My wife's health is important to me."

"Of course. And the baby is born, I assume?"

"Yes. A healthy boy, eleven months already."

"Congratulations. Now, Mister Shaw. Tell the court weather you recognize this firearm."

"Allow the witness to inspect this weapon. Do you recognize this firearm?"

"Yes. It is mine."

"According to forensic reports, the round that killed Brendon Shaw, was discharged from this firearm."

"Now, Mister Shaw, about this murder weapon. How did a firearm registered in your name got into the possession of the accused?"

"I wish I could explain that, but I have no idea."

"Where was the weapon the last time you saw it?"

"It was locked in the safe of my brother, Brendon."

"Explain to the court why was your firearm in your brother's safe."

"I am a registered dealer in firearms and ammunition. Brendon was also interested in firearms. We often went to the range for target practicing together. A few days before he was shot, I showed him a couple of firearms and he picked that one for our next practice session. I let him keep it in his safe until we went to the range the next Saturday."

"No further Questions from the state." The defense attorney got up and looked at the jury before he started his questioning.

"Mister Shaw, were you and your brother, the victim close?"

"We were as close as brothers can be.'

"Did you always, without exception agree on everything?"

"Not on everything, no."

"Did you ever argue?"

"Sometimes, I guess; like brothers sometimes do."

"Did you ever threaten him?"

"I did not.'

"Did you, or did you not tell him the day before the murder that sometimes he makes you so mad you can kill him?"

"I didn't use the word 'kill'. I said I could throttle him."

"Can a person die when throttled?"

"I don't know. I'm not a pathologist."

"Would you have liked to throttle your brother to death if it were possible?"

"Of course not. I don't know where you're going with this."

"It is for me to know and for you to answer the questions." Here the judge cut in saying:

"I surely don't understand the purpose of your questioning. Please get on with it. Just keep in mind, Mr. Shaw is not on trial."

"Just trying to establish motive, your Honor. No further questions."

* * * *

"Mrs. Shaw, please tell the court when was the last time you saw your husband alive."

"I danced with him on the patio. Later he went inside, some friends came to talk to me and we also went inside. The temperature was dropping and people preferred not to hang around outside anymore. I did not see my husband after that."

"But someone saw your husband go outside again and saw you following him. Isn't that right?"

"I was looking for my husband. Some of the guests asked me where he was, so I went looking for him."

"On the patio, where there was no one?"

"I looked everywhere, not just on the patio."

"Did you find him?"

"No, I already said I didn't see him after I danced with him earlier."

"Do you know the combination to the safe, Mrs. Shaw?"

Her hesitation was hardly noticeable.

"No. I do not," she replied with confidence.

"Is it not unusual for a wife not to know the combination of the safe in her own house?"

"What do you mean? No, it is not unusual. The safe was used for Brendon's work. I had no use for it."

"And you were never curious? You never tried to find out what was in the safe, or what the combination might be?"

"No. I had no reason to." She kept her sweating hands in her lap, out of sight, for fear they might start trembling.

"Thank you Mrs Shaw, you may step down."

* * * *

During the next days some witnesses among staff members were called to the stand to testify to the relationship between their employer and themselves, his wife and also whether it were possible for any of them to get into the safe. It was established that in general Brendon was a good and fair employer, not patient and not tolerant of mistakes, a bit short fused at times, but willing to listen to problems and make the means available to handle those problems quickly and efficiently. Someone insinuated that he was abusive to his wife, but neither the prosecution nor the defense pursued the matter. It was also established that it was highly improbable but not impossible for any employee, household or otherwise, to acquire access to the safe. Security measures were always in place and never neglected. Of course nothing is totally foolproof.

On the last day of the trial, the accused was called in for cross-examination.

"Your Honor, I ran when the police arrived, because the butler and the gardener are always the first suspects."

"Only in fiction, Mr. Davies. What were you doing in the garden at that late hour? Or do you always do your gardening late at night when your employer has a party going?"

"I was checking on the movement detector lights. I couldn't sleep, so I went for a walk. I saw some lights were not working, so I went closer to inspect."

"How do you explain your fingerprints on the murder weapon?"

"I found the gun lying in a flower bed next to a garden light. I was curious and picked it up."

"Don't you know you are not supposed to pick up a murder weapon?"

"I did not know at the time it was a murder weapon."

"Oh, right. Guns are lying around in the garden all the time!"

"No, they don't. That's why I was curious.'

"So, when did you find out it was a murder weapon?"

"Objection!"

"Answer the question."

"I heard sirens and as I turned around, I saw Mr. Shaw lying in the rosebush."

"What happened then?"

"I dropped the gun and ran."

"Why did you run away? If you were not guilty, why did you run?"

"I panicked. People were approaching, the police; it looked like the whole police force, was storming in, and there I was close to a man, obviously shot, with a weapon in my hand? What was I supposed to do, call them saying 'hi guys, here is a man in a bush, he has been shot and here is a weapon,' is that what you would have done?"

"Stop the conjecture and answer the questions. Where were the paramedics at that time?"

"I don't know. Maybe they were still on their way."

"You are lying. The paramedics were there first. You waited until they left so that you could retrieve the murder weapon before the homicide detectives arrive."

"Objection, your Honor, leading the witness."

"Sustained. Stick to cross-examination. That means you ask questions and the defendant answers."

"Did you wait for the paramedics to leave so that you could retrieve the murder weapon?"

"No, I was inspecting the lights."

"And you didn't see or hear the paramedics in spite of the noise of their own sirens? You expect the court to believe that?"

"I don't expect you to believe anything, you stupid jerk," he mumbled.

"Speak up, Mr. Davies, the court needs to hear what you say."

"Sorry your Honor. I said I was probably still on the other side of the garden at the time. The music from the house was loud. Maybe that's why I didn't hear the paramedics."

"Your Honor, where is this line of questioning leading? My we ask that prosecution stick to facts and not conjecture?"

"Defence so ordered. Proceed."

"Your Honor, I'm trying to establish the chain of events of the night of the murder."

"I think that has already been done, Mr. Hawkins."

"Right. Mr. Davies, what did you do when you saw Mr. Shaw lying in the bush? Why didn't you call for help?"

"I would have, if the police were not already storming in."

"Are you sure it is not because you already knew he was dead?"

"Objection!"

"Sustained."

"Did you know he was dead?"

"I did not."

"Do you really expect the court to believe you? You did not see the paramedics, yet their presence was obvious to everyone else. You know, red lights flickering, lighting up the place. You did not hear the paramedics because the music was too loud. Let me tell you how I see it. You shot Mr. Shaw in cold blood. Mr. Crawford came out on the patio and saw movement in the shadows, so you hid behind a bush hoping you'd get away. But, as Mr. Crawford has already testified, he went out to inspect. That was when he found the body and alerted the police. While you were hiding, you realized you had somehow lost the gun with your fingerprints on it. You tried to retrieve the gun, but there were people all over the place and the patrolman and the paramedics arrived minutes later. Only after the patrolman cleared the scene of onlookers, and the paramedics left, you took the only chance you had to retrieve the gun. Unfortunately the time-window was not long enough to get the gun and get away. You, Mr. Davies, shot and killed the victim. You made a widow of a young woman who thought she had a future with the man she loved!"

Half raised from his seat on the stand, Floyd Davies, gripping the wooden railing in front of him, said in a loud voice: "Yes! I killed him. I killed the bastard. I did not make a widow, I rid the world of a vicious, cruel abuser. Mrs. Shaw can go to bed at night knowing no one will ever hurt her again. I love her. I couldn't stand him hurting her anymore!"

Minutes passed in complete silence, before the prosecutor said: "No more questions, your Honor."

Floyd Davies was found guilty and sentenced to twenty-five years in prison. How he got hold of the murder weapon will forever remain a mystery. Or not.

CHAPTER 3

The prisoner

He swung his backpack off his shoulder and dropped it on the table. Home. A kitchenette with breakfast-nook, living room, bedroom, bathroom. Furniture not new, but good quality. Tastefully decorated. He walked through the cottage opening windows as he went. Enough space for all his stuff, and to spare. Cupboards in the bedroom provided more space than he might ever need. Kitchenette, fully fitted, the same, with all the equipment to make life comfortable.

All he needed, was provisions. But, opening the kitchen cupboards, he realized even that was provided. Just basics, though, he was thankful, nevertheless. There was coffee grounds, a French plunger, sugar, tea, even hot chocolate. There were also a small variety of spreads, crackers, containers with rice, pasta and a number of canned meats, fish and vegetables. The fridge was stocked with eggs, butter, cheese and fresh cream. How is that for welcoming a new employee. After looking around some more, he rinsed the kettle, switched it on, rinsed the plunger and found a mug.

Mug with steaming coffee in hand he carried his backpack to the bedroom and shook the contents out on the bed. Time to unpack. Toiletry bag to the bathroom, yesterday's change of clothing in the laundry basket; the rest got hung in the wardrobe or stacked in the shelves; under-ware in the drawers. He took his time packing everything in its proper place and tidying up the room. After he took a shower, he put his dirty clothes in the washer, spread some crackers on a plate, scrambled eggs, emptied a can of salmon on top of everything and sat down at the breakfast-nook.

Kitchen clean, laundry in the dryer, his hunger satisfied, Floyd Davies sat down in an easy chair and studied his work-contract. Mr. Shaw insisted he take another day to get settled in before starting to work. The next day was Friday, so he would start on Monday. He went systematically through the contract to make sure he did not miss anything. Not that it would matter now, it was signed already. He put down the contract on the side table, took the newspaper, page through it and fell asleep. It had been a long day of travelling, finalizing his employment arrangements, some more travelling and at last his tired body and soul gave way at the moment of realization that he was now allowed to rest. That he had a place to stay, a place, though not his own, where he can come home to, relax and not worry where he will put down his head the following evening.

* * * *

Deadly Innocent

Floyd Davies spent the weekend settling in and to explore the three-acre plot that was now his responsibility. He also acquainted himself with some of the other staff members and the workers under his supervision. There were three permanent gardeners, who would take orders from him and report to him. They all lived in and their quarters, a short distance from his own, right next to those of the four permanent cleaners and two cooks, who reported to Mrs. Brown, the housekeeper. She was a big, friendly, person who ran the household, from the cooking and cleaning to the laundry and everything else concerning household matters. Mrs. Brown did not live in the staff quarters. She was burdened with the privilege of living in a suite inside the main house.

Early on Monday morning Floyd called his workers together, opened the meeting with the reading of a short Psalm from the Bible, said a short prayer and officially took his place as head of the gardening and maintenance team. He quickly directed his team to their duties for the day. As soon as they left, each one to his allocated task, Floyd sat down in the little office and went through the paperwork to see what his predecessor left him. His new life had begun. A life of permanent employment in the line of work that he enjoyed most. Gardening and maintenance.

The first week passed quickly, as did the whole first month. He kept busy, made sure his staff did what was expected and found satisfaction in the fact that he had full authority to do as he pleased as long as he kept everything in perfect order and create a beautiful garden where the people of the house can relax and refresh their weary souls. The garden was a bit too formal and boring to his taste. So, the first project he laid on himself was to design a complete new landscape, starting at the back of the house, just east of the staff quarters, working his way round the house to the front right down to the edge where land met ocean.

Design in place, cost calculated, Floyd Davies started working on his new project with great enthusiasm. Making small changes first, as he did not want to upset everyone with big changes right away, he moved a few flowerbeds carefully making sure the plants were not damaged. He did not like to destroy life, however insignificant, even the tiniest plant had to be handled with care. This principal he impressed on his workers every day.

Some flowerbeds had to be relocated to make space for a pathway to a gazebo on the north-east side of the house. It was easy for him to imagine the lady of the house, Mrs. Shaw, walking down the pathway through fragrant shrubs to go and sit in the gazebo with a good book and enjoy some alone-time away from it all. He was planning to make the surroundings of this gazebo as tranquil as he possibly could. A water feature close by must be a focal point. Enclosed with shrubs and tall, flowering plants, surrounded by smaller flowers, complemented with groundcovers placed in a-symmetrical patterns all around the little refuge for peace and quiet, she was the inspiration for the design.

Floyd Davies had met Penelope Shaw only once before he started working there. She happened to be near the side door when he reported for his first interview. On his first ringing of the doorbell, she opened and invited him in. She was not overly friendly, but not businesslike either. Only the beginning of a smile touched the corners of her mouth as she offered her hand, her dark brown eyes looked straight into his without wavering. Her dark brown hair was caught loosely in a cream colored clip behind her head, just above the nape of her neck. She was wearing a wine-red sundress and black low-heal summer sandals, displaying tiny, well-pedicured feet. Short of breath, he followed her gracious, ballerina-like walk as she led the way to Mr. Shaw's office down the hall. The impression she made on him, would stay with him forever. Many of the changes in the garden's design, was inspired by those few moments in her presence.

* * * *

At the back of his cottage, was a small piece of garden, neglected and waiting for the right man to make a change. Floyd considered it to be the ideal place to cultivate a vegetable garden for himself. He had always dreamt of growing his own food, but the years on the road prevented it. At last he got the opportunity to grow whatever vegetables he could fit into that small space.

Weekdays he worked the big garden, Saturdays he spent all day in his own little haven. First of all, he fenced it in. To utilize every inch of space, he planted all the climbing vegetables against the chain-link fence he had put up around his backyard. Tomatoes, green-beans, cucumbers, squash, and closer to the cottage he made beds where he planted carrots, beets, cabbage, lettuce, leeks and many more of his favorites. Although it was already summer, there was still enough warm-weather days left to have a harvest of the summer veg.

* * * *

Floyd was examining a cluster of shrubs close to the house. He spotted what looked like the first signs of a fungus on the leaves when it happened. Voices, angry voices. They were coming from a room less than ten feet from where he was standing. Then there was a scream, a crash, something breaking and Brendon Shaw saying: "That will teach you". He heard Mrs. Shaw whimpering, groaning and then it was quiet.

He was stunned. Couldn't move, couldn't think. What he had heard a moment ago, was a complete surprise. A very unpleasant one. What on earth was that? All through his life he had met many men who were abusive towards their wives and children. Abuse was nothing new. But these two people simply didn't fit the cast. Mrs. Shaw was so dainty, like a fragile porcelain doll. And Mr. Shaw seemed so refined, so in control. Never before had he misjudged anyone that badly. He did not know it at the time, but it would be his first witnessing of many incidents of that kind.

During the months that followed, Floyd made a point of watching his employers. Mr. Shaw travelled a lot and when he was away, Floyd kept his distance from the house. There was enough work along the perimeter of the property to avoid ever coming close to where he knew Mrs. Shaw would be. She hardly ever wandered further than about a hundred steps away, smelling the roses or sit in the gazebo, as he knew she would. She never went to the beach alone.

Whenever Mr. Shaw was at home, Floyd would always find a reason to work near the house. He kept his eyes and ears open and often heard or saw what he knew he would, but shouldn't. It pained him to have to listen to her pleading for mercy, just to hear her being slapped or punched, but he couldn't help himself. He had to be close to her when that vicious animal was around. It took all his self-control not to storm in and throttle the man. How can anyone touch that sweet, delicate woman in any way but lovingly? If there were only something he could do. But he dared not interfere. All he could do was pray.

Mrs. Shaw spent more time in the garden towards the end of summer. The air was fresh and cool. Each time they exchanged a few words. She would ask him something about his work, a specific flower, or what he was planning for the next season and he would politely answer her question. One day he asked her a question and immediately realized his mistake: "Mrs. Shaw ... "

"Please, I know your name is Floyd. Just call me Penelope."

"Mrs., eh, Penelope, I can't help but notice the blue patch on the side of your face. Did you fall of bump into something?" She touched her sunglasses as if she tried to hide the sickly blue mark with it.

"Mr. Davies, sorry for keeping you. I shouldn't be bothering you while you are working. Good day, Floyd."

But the next day she was back, without the sunglasses. They chatted for a few minutes, not mentioning anything about the previous day. And so the first few weeks of fall passed with pleasant, though short conversations, almost daily. He got to know a little about her likes and dislikes; he told her a lot about his veg garden and she was quite impressed. He pulled a young carrot from the soil, washed it and gave it to her to taste. She told him she had never tasted a carrot as sweet as that one.

With the change of the seasons, he saw less of both of them. They spent less time in the garden and went out with friends more often. The basics of what he planned to do in the garden were more or less in place. Come spring, he would finish the work of redesigning and landscaping. He spent less time in the garden and more time maintaining the buildings. He had to find a way to be close to her and small problems in the house gave him the convenient excuse to do just that, but never did he enter the house when Brendon Shaw was not there.

* * * *

While in the house he was often subjected to observing the abuse. The sudden loud voice, the scream followed by sounds that could be anything from something falling over, breaking, to Penelope falling after a slap or a punch, followed by sounds of crying and the next day the excuses, the apologies, the pampering and the gifts delivered to the house resultant of the abusing husband's feelings of guilt. Worst of all were the lies to friends and family: Penelope is accident-prone. Penelope is clumsy. She slipped and fell. She bumped into … whatever he could think of at that moment. There was no telling who believed him and who didn't. Those who believed him sympathized. It must be hard to have a wife who was permanently injured in some way. Those who didn't, simply ignored it and did nothing to help or support Penelope or put a stop to it.

He was in the kitchen with Maggie Brown to fix a light switch one day when they both heard the usual sounds of abuse. Floyd said nothing, but Maggie Brown folded her arms across her large bosom and muttered the words that had come to his mind often before: "Someday, someday someone is going to do something about that." She looked meaningfully at him, then turned away to switch on the kettle. Before he finished the work in the kitchen, she poured them both a cup of tea and placed a bowl of biscuits on the table.

"How long has this been going on?" he asked, sitting at the table across from her.

"Ever since they got married six, almost seven years ago."

"And no one knows except us?"

"She has a sister in Canada who visits once in a while. I think she suspects something. But what can she do about it? Mr. Shaw will not tolerate interference. Not even from his sister-in-law."

"Why do abused women stay?"

"That is a mystery we might never be able to solve. But something has changed in her eyes. I would not be surprised if she decides to leave him. Soon."

"You might be right. I have also noticed a kind of coldness that sometimes creeps into her eyes. A hardness you would not normally associate with someone as gentle as her."

"The place will not be the same without her, but I hope she does it. The sooner, the better."

"What about his brother? Is the other Mr. Shaw also ...?"

"Nooo. You can't find a more decent human being on this earth."

"Do you think he knows about all this?"

"He surely must know his brother has a temper. But I don't know whether he realizes what is going on. Brendon is an excellent liar and often good people are too naive to believe anything bad about other people." The sound of footsteps descending on the stairway cautioned them. Floyd swallowed the last bit of tea, stuffed a biscuit into his mouth and left. Maggie Brown got up and cleared the cups. Brendon didn't enter the kitchen, he had no reason to, just went out through the front door, got into his car and drove away. Tonight I will send supper up to Penelope's suite, Maggie thought. She will not show her face down here for a day or two.

Winter passed and spring arrived with a burst of new life. Floyd finished his most important project of redoing the garden. His employers were very pleased, paid him a big bonus and invited friends and family to a party to celebrate the new look. Naturally Floyd Davies, the gardener was not invited. You just don't party with your employees. Mrs. Shaw did mention his name and told a small group of people that it was all his idea and how privileged they were to have him. One of this group mentioned it later to Brendon and made him frown.

Later that night when the party had broken up and all the guests had gone home, Brendon confronted her. The explanation she presented was not good enough for him. He threw a half-empty wine bottle at her, hitting her in the face and splashing wine all over her. The moment she hit the floor, he was there and started slapping her over and over. Only half conscious, she crawled in under the table in the dining room where it was not easy to reach her. Maggie Brown was in her bathroom when she heard the commotion. She went to investigate and found Penelope lying under the table and Brendon standing next to it.

"She lost an earring. It must have rolled under the table." He was too quick with an explanation. She realized instantly what was happening.

"Go to bed Sir, I'll help her look for the earring."

"No, no it's OK. You can go back to bed."

"Sir, it's no problem. I'll help her," Maggie said with a stern face. But Brendon did not back down. He knew too well Maggie would see the injuries to Penelope's face. He didn't want that. In a gentler, controlled voice he replied: "Really, Mrs. Brown, don't worry, we'll have a look in the morning. It's not that important." To his wife he said gently: "Come on, Honey, let's go to bed. If we don't find it tomorrow, I'll buy you another pair." Maggie Brown turned and left without a word.

* * * *

Through careful observation Floyd learned how things worked in the household. He learned that there was no pattern behind the abuse. Brendon exploded at any amount of provocation. He exploded at no provocation at all. It all depended on the mood and mindset he was in and his own personal perception of a situation. Breaking routine, Penelope being absent from the house when he arrived at home and surprise guests were among the situations that carried a high risk for an explosion. Besides those, there were a number of other things, small, insignificant things that might or might not aggravate him to a point of starting an argument which might or might not end in physical violence.

Floyd also learned personal things about both Brendon Shaw and Penelope Shaw; their interests, Brendon's line of business and Penelope's friendship circles. Brendon's Brother Simon was a firearm expert and they often exchanged guns, of which they both had quite an impressive collection. They often went target shooting together. More than once, Penelope insisted on accompanying them, totally against Brendon's wishes. Simon convinced him that their women didn't see enough of their husbands and he agreed to let Penelope and Tilda tag along once in a while.

Not only did he learn who their friends were, but their enemies as well. Greg Atwood was number one on that list. Some of the partners were not fond of Brendon, but one could not consider them enemies. And then there was a rival company that could not stop the rumor of a planned takeover. Floyd suspected Brendon's informant brought bad news on the night of Penelope's birthday party. That might have been the reason he stormed out onto the patio, into the garden. A Killer had been waiting for him and was taken by surprise when someone else appeared on the scene and pulled a trigger.

At night in his cell, Floyd constantly pondered these events that landed him behind bars. There were too many unanswered questions. Too many hows and whys and too few answers. What would have happened if he didn't pick up the gun in the garden? How many sets of fingerprints would have been identified on the gun if he didn't rub it clean? What would have happened if he didn't "confess" to the murder? Where would the case have ended if he just kept answering the questions truthfully?

Everything he said in court was the truth. Everything, except his "confession". Nothing was more true than when he said: "I love her". In the dark of night it was the image of her face that he saw when falling asleep. When he woke up in the morning, her image as she walked around in the garden, was what encouraged him to go through the routine. In the heat of the day, he recalled the pleasure of her tasting a carrot or cucumber from his garden. At such moments he worked harder to make a success of his veg garden here on the prison grounds. Twenty-five years with the possibility of parole. By the end of that, his garden might be producing enough to feed the whole prison, staff included.

CHAPTER 4

A New Life

The widow of Brendon Shaw appropriately mourned for three months. She stayed mostly at home, did only a little shopping when necessary, had lunch with a friend or two in a humble coffee shop once a week, received only close friends and family who dropped in once in a while. Otherwise she stayed in her private quarters contemplating the guilty plea. Was Floyd Davies really in love with her? How did prison-life treat him? Was he an outcast? Was he a hero among his inmates for killing to protect an abused woman? Was he vulnerable because of his age? He was after all not as old as she thought. His weatherworn face made him look much older than his forty-seven years, which meant he was only nineteen years older than her. It was a big age difference, but not too big for him to fall in love with someone her age.

In her private wing of the eleven-bedroom mansion, she also spent much time planning her future. She was not penniless when she married Brendon Shaw, but Penelope, as his main heir, would soon be a very wealthy woman. Young, stunningly beautiful, and rich beyond most people's dreams would make her a target for prowlers. She knew that. Planning ahead was the only way to prevent her from falling into a trap worse than the one she had just escaped.

Penelope Watson was young, just graduated from college and looking forward to starting a career in teaching home-economics when she met Brendon, was swept off her feet, married him within two months and moved with him to his New York apartment in Manhattan. Three years later he bought a house in Greenwich Village where they lived for almost two years. They relocated to East Hampton on Long Island and about a year after they moved in, Floyd Davies was appointed gardener and maintenance manager.

The beatings started as soon as the honeymoon was over. Brendon lost his temper at the slightest provocation. And sometimes at no provocation at all. Physical abuse, however bad, was not the worst Penelope had to endure. She could not decide which was worse, a black eye and bruised ribs or the humiliation in front of strangers.

"Penny, I want you to do something special for yourself. Go to a spa or beauty parlor and have a treat. You need it." She had made a small mistake with something he asked her to do. They were still living in Manhattan at the time. Expecting a whipping, Penny apologized over and over until he quietened her: "Enough, Penny. I'm getting it. You said you're sorry and I accept it. Everyone can make a mistake. You do make a lot more mistakes than anyone I know, but I love you and I have to live with your mistakes, don't I? Now, take this credit card and tomorrow you go out and enjoy yourself." He handed her a card, kissed her on the forehead and retreated to his study.

Knowing how easily he got upset when she wandered too far away to his liking, she chose a beauty parlor close to home, as he would not be going to his office in town, but rather work from home. Being constantly nervous as a way of life, it was not easy for her to relax. Halfway through the treatment, though, she managed to lean back and push Brendon to the back of her mind. This is how life was supposed to be, she told herself, convinced that Brendon regretted his treatment of her and that he might change his conduct towards her.

Then it was time to pay, to use the credit card he gave her. It was declined. She asked the cashier to run it again, again it was declined. As she was about to call Brendon on her cell phone, he stepped into the parlor and said loud enough for everyone to hear: "Oh, there you are. I wondered where you'd go." Clicking his tongue, he continued: "Running off with my credit card like that. Naughty, naughty girl." To the staff members who were present he said: "Sorry ladies, my wife has a tendency to pinch one of my credit cards and clear out the shops. I cannot allow that anymore, so I cancelled all but the one I use most. Just can't afford it anymore." He put his arm around her shoulders and led her out, saying, still loudly: "Come on Honey, let me take you home so you can burn supper for me."

She was a fast learner. A few months later he tried the same trick on her, but she was ready. Very carefully she swopped the credit card he gave her for one that had unlimited credit. Very early the next day she went to the most expensive art gallery within walking distance from his down-town office, knowing he would be there all morning. Also, knowing he would not be able to follow her because she heard him talking on the phone about at least two important meetings with partners and some clients, expecting her to do her shopping in the afternoon.

As the second meeting was about to begin, she walked into his office, charmingly apologized to everyone telling them ever so sweetly that she needed just a minute with her husband.

"No, please, gentlemen, don't leave. I'll be just a minute and then I'll be off. You see, my dear husband here was so generous as to give me his credit card telling me to get myself something special. But nothing gives me more pleasure than to buy him nice things. So what do you all think?" She then produced two paintings from a container she had been carrying: "Darling, I know how much you love the work of this artist, and when I saw these two paintings, I just had to buy them for your office." She kissed him on the cheek and said: "Right gentlemen, I'm done. Thanks for your patience. Enjoy your meeting. Bye Sweetheart." Gracefully, ever so gracefully she left the office, smiled at the receptionist and walked out the door.

By the time she reached the sidewalk, Penny was shivering for fear that something might go wrong, hoping her act was convincing. But tonight I'll have to face him, and who knows what mood he'll be in, she thought. Perhaps he would realize she swopped the credit card. He never made mistakes like that. For deceit like that, she'll pay dearly. And then, spending tens of thousands of Dollars on the most horrible paintings might bring on the ultimate punishment. He didn't mind spending money on good art, but it had to be good. He certainly wouldn't appreciate her getting back at him like that.

Penny needed coffee to help her recover and to work out a plan to avoid a beating. She ducked into the nearest coffee shop and ordered a double espresso. With the steaming coffee in front of her, she took out her cell phone and dialed a number.

"Tilda, hi, I was wondering if you and Simon would like to come over tonight? Just for cocktails? Super, see you then." She dialed another and another number and got two more couples willing and eager to visit. Perhaps, after a hard day at the office and cocktails afterward Brendon would be too tired to spend energy beating her up.

She was wrong. After everyone had left, she excused herself and went up to her quarters. Taking off her earrings, her back was turned to the door when he rushed in. He grabbed her by the hair and threw her against a wall. He screamed at her never to make a fool of him like that again and stormed out. At least she was partially right about him being tired. If he wasn't, it might have been much worse. She could feel there was little strength in his arm as he tried to smash her against the wall. She hardly felt the blow. Lucky me, she thought. He even forgot to ask back his credit card.

But all that was in the past. Penelope focused on creating herself a new future. She sold the house in East Hampton, bought an apartment in Manhattan, and stayed there for the rest of the year. She would keep it only for her visits to New York once a year. Now it was time to make drastic changes. Early in January of the following year, she packed one bag, locked the door and asked the cab driver to take her to the airport. Almost a week earlier she had booked a seat on a flight to New Orleans, the place of her birth.

It was not hard to find a good place to stay. After viewing a few houses, she found just what she was looking for, bought it, furnished it, and moved in. As there was nothing in the house, it was time to do a little shopping. Bedding linen, towels, kitchen equipment, she took her time choosing everything she never had the privilege to choose. Brendon had designers and staff to do that. Slowly and carefully she went about decorating the place to her taste and quite enjoyed it. Although she could afford the best, the most expensive, she did not bother to show off her wealth. She bought what she liked, whether it came from a One-Dollar-Store or the most exclusive shop in town made no difference. Quite a few items were acquired while browsing flea markets. Stage one was finished. The next step was a visit to a car dealer.

This was the only luxury she allowed herself. After test driving several models of luxury cars, she finally chose a bright red sporty BMW. Penelope could easily have chosen a super-fast Italian car, but had no taste for those. Very proud of herself she took her maiden drive around town in her shiny little roadster, hood off in spite of the slight chill in the wind.

The highway to Biloxi, route 90 was, as expected, not busy. The weather was partly cloudy with a slight breeze from the ocean; temperature just over sixty; thirty percent chance of precipitation according to the radio forecast. She enjoyed the early morning drive, breathing in the fresh air after so many years of stale New York smog. Without the desire to push the car to its limits, she drove along unhurriedly soaking in the freedom to do as she pleased. It was a long forgotten feeling that she had to get acquainted to all over again. Close to midtown Biloxi she took an exit from the highway, went north, turned right and left and parked in front of a neat white house.

Her mother was waiting in the doorway by the time she got out of the car. They embraced each other on the small front lawn.

"Elma, is it our little girl?" came a familiar voice from inside the house. Then the huge figure of her father appeared in the doorway. He bear hugged his daughter and stood aside so the women can go in before him.

"You look pale. And thin" her mother commented as soon as they sat down by the kitchen table.

"What you've been through, it's no wonder. But the fresh air here by the coast will do you good. Are you really back for good?"

"Yes, Daddy. I won't be going back to New York any time soon. And if I do, it will be for a brief visit, nothing more. I have friends there. Good friends whom I'll miss. But they understand why I couldn't stay. Maybe some of them will visit me in New Orleans." Her mother placed a cup of coffee in front of her and gave one to her husband and placed in the middle of the table a large bowl of home baked goodies. Then she sat down with her own coffee and said: "Now, tell us everything. If you want to talk about it, of course." She started giving them the short version of what had happened. Most of the detail was left out. Like how much she enjoyed the garden and talking to Floyd, the gardener. She left out the abuse, the humiliation. She left out the part how she tried to figure a way out of the marriage. She took what was reported in the media and elaborated on that. It might not be enough for them, but for now it will have to do, she thought.

"At least the guy who murdered your husband is behind bars now. He won't kill again. Hopefully he won't get parole."

"But that man, the murderer, what's his name? Floyd, or something. He said you were abused. Is that true?"

"Daddy, please, I don't want to talk about it anymore."

"Is it true?" her father asked slowly, looking her directly in the eyes. She nodded, looked away.

"Yes, Brendon hurt me. Often." Penelope could hear her mother gasped in disbelief. Her father said: "If I had known I would have done it. I would have pulled the trigger and blast the bastard away from this planet."

"I know. That's why I never told you."

"Why didn't you divorce him? I still can't believe it. He seemed such a nice boy."

"Elma, looks are deceiving. We only saw him at the wedding. Remember, he always had an excuse not to visit, neither would he let Penelope visit us. That should have set the red lights flickering. I should have known something was not right."

"Daddy, how's your back? Looks like you move around easier now?" This question was their cue that the subject is closed and it was time to move on to something else. She stayed with them for two more days, dodging their questions, telling as little as possible and just enjoying their company for the first time in many years. If only her sister were also there. She missed Pricilla so much since they moved to Canada.

* * * *

It was a blissful summer. Penelope made full use of the fine weather, going places, making new friends, most of the old friends had moved away, but those who were still there, renewed their friendships with her and made her feel at home again. Very few people connected her with Brandon, the murder, the trial and few knew she used to be Mrs. Shaw because she had taken back her maiden name. She was just Penny Watson again.

With the beginning of the new academic year, Penny Watson registered at the university for a course in financial management. Brendon had taught her well not to trust anyone with money without even knowing it. He thought she had no sense and no other use than to look pretty. He never realized how closely she watched him, listened when he spoke to his partners, clients and other business associates. She learned a lot, but not enough. Her wealth was being managed for her by someone else, but she wanted to take control of it sooner or later.

* * * *

With several degrees in business, trade and commerce she felt qualified to enter and be counted in the world of finance. During her study years, she spent much time at the offices of her managers in New York, learning from them the tricks of the trade. Knowledge alone is not good enough. To gain experience she had to work and see how things work practically. After a week with her parents during each summer holiday, she would pack her bags and fly to New York for a working holiday. And in the process she healed, gained back her confidence, her self-esteem, her personality. She grew as a person in every aspect of her being.

Slowly and patiently, Penelope Watson took control over her assets, one at a time. One by one, she incorporated all that was previously owned and ruled over by Brendon into her own company, wiping out everything that was associated with the Shaw name. It took eight years to obliterate the name of Brendon Shaw from the world of finance and consume the company that took him twelve years to build.

She could finally sit back and say to herself time had come to start taking it easy, to relax and enjoy what she had worked for. All those grueling years of study and work, then her slowly taking over, which meant working even harder, finally paid off. Penelope Watson was now in charge. Penelope Watson had replaced Brendon Shaw. She had taken back what he stole from her, all the while feeling lucky as if someone was praying for her.

CHAPTER 5

Parole

Floyd Davies was a model prisoner. In eighteen years he was never in trouble, never had a scuffle with an inmate, was never impolite with a guard, never complained. Parole was a given. Just over eighteen years after the iron bars clanged and the keys crunched in the locks behind him, closing him in for a time that then, felt like eternity, he was a free man. He walked out of prison with a bag full of clothing, a few books, pictures and a file filled with newspaper clippings. Those were all he possessed this side of the barbed wire fence.

There was no one to pick him up. Because there never was anyone for him. After Angie and Jamie, Floyd had no one. Father and mother long gone, brother died in Iraq, no sisters, Floyd was alone. He started walking. For years he never thought of Angie. He managed to wipe her memory from his mind for months at a time, then, suddenly there she was, vividly smiling in his thoughts. And every time it was as painful as ever. Minutes after the caskets was lowered into the ground, one on top of the other, Floyd took off never to be seen in the small town of Concordia, Iowa again.

He forced his thoughts back to the presence. Eighteen years was enough time to formulate a plan for this day. Yet, as he strode along, it felt strange. He prepared for this day, but now that it had come, it was not what he anticipated. Of course he knew it would not be so. Those inmates who were in and out, told many stories of how weird it was to be free again. For some it was an anti-climax. For others it was their happiest day. Floyd never asked why they didn't make sure not to lose their freedom again. There would not be any logical answer.

Again he had to check his thoughts. There were things he had to do. It would be best to focus on that, instead of letting his mind wander to things in the past. His planning of that day was perfectly in place. All he had to do, was to go according to his plans and to do what needed to be done.

* * * *

It was an easy job, tending the gardens of the city parks under supervision of the full-time landscaper. He did not, however, do all the work himself. Much of the work was delegated to younger men whom he had to supervise. But standing still, watching others do all the work had never been one of his strengths. He often, even at his age, now sixty-five, jumped in and help getting the job done faster. Just like it was in his young days. After college he worked for a gardening company, one of many. He was the most diligent worker and never complained. With his qualifications and experience he knew exactly what to do.

Two years after starting his own gardening business, he met Angie. She was the daughter of one of his clients. Having graduated from college where she studied bookkeeping, she was looking for a job close to home. He needed a bookkeeper. Though it was part of his training, he did not have the knack for it. They fell in love, married, worked together in their gardening business, he doing the physical work with the help of seasonal casuals, she running the office. They rented a two-bedroom house and started a family a year later. Jamie was a perfect little boy, the joy of his parents and Angie's father, who spent time with him whenever he was free. Jamie was the son he never had.

Jamie had just started school when Angie's father died of a heart attack. The day before the funeral, Angie insisted to fetch Jamie from school as she in fact, did every day. Snow was melting and there was ice on the roads. Floyd argued with her, telling her just to wait for him to finish a bit of planning for the next season, it wouldn't take a minute, but she wouldn't listen. She did not want Jamie to wait. When the school bell rang, she had to be there.

On their way back, two blocks from their house, she tried to pass a double-parked car. Indicating her intent, she waited her turn and as she started moving into the left lane, another vehicle came from behind, cut her off, leaving her open to an oncoming truck. The truck hit the brakes, skidded on the ice, lost control and slammed into Angie's car, almost flattening it against the parked car. They were both killed instantly. Angie and Jamie would not attend her father's funeral. They would have their own, two days later.

* * * *

Life went smoothly on for Floyd Davies. Early every morning he turned up for work, fell asleep in front of the TV at night, and met with his parole officer once a week. In the beginning, the officer visited him at his workplace randomly and without prior notice. After a year the parole officer, Randy Boyd slacked down because Floyd never set foot outside his routine, never gave any cause for concern. The weekly checks became monthly checks. Just like he was a model prisoner, he was then a model parolee.

Randy later even skipped some of the monthly checks. He knew it was not right, but lazy as he was, he did not think with such a perfect case anyone would care or even notice.

Since he lived modestly on necessities, including no luxuries on his shopping lists, he managed to save from his small salary. After two years on parole he had a fair sum of money stashed. Weekends he spent in internet cafes surfing the internet. In prison he learned how to find everything on Google. He also learned about social media. It was so easy to keep track of Penelope and every development in her life. He often wondered what he would feel when he saw her again.

CHAPTER 6

Love Rekindled

Penelope, married eight years earlier, divorced five years later, lived alone, minding her business, had become a creature of habit in some ways. Every morning she would go for a jog, shower and head down town to have breakfast in a coffee shop near her office. Over a second cup of coffee, she would read the early edition and then go to the office to start the day's business.

That morning it was no different. She just started her second cup of coffee.

"My I have a seat. Please." Though the coffee shop was not full, she looked up to see a man standing by her table. Did she hear correctly? Did he ask to sit at her table? With lifted eyebrows she started to ask him why, then checked herself. This man looked so familiar. She shrugged and he sat down.

"Mrs. Shaw, Penelope Shaw, may I ask how you are?" His hands rested on the table in front of him. She looked puzzled at him. Why did he address her as Mrs. Shaw? The hands. She looked at the hands. Couldn't help but notice them, recognize them.

"Floyd Davies! How on earth?" She paled at the realization that Floyd Davies was no longer locked away. He was free and sitting across the table from her, less than three feet away. She had never been closer to him than this. What did he want from her?

"Yes. You remember."

"How can I not remember you?"

"Of course. Are you all right?"

"I'm fine. You?"

"As you see. Fit as a fiddle. Free and going places."

"I'm so glad. Are you travelling through or staying in town?" She was still holding the newspaper as if she might want to keep on reading, but folded it when Floyd ordered coffee.

"I'll be in town for a few days. Then I'll have to run back before my parole officer misses me." The words came easy. He thought it would be hard to talk to her about prison, parole and all that.

"When did you get out?" She took a sip from her cup, now cold, pushed it aside and ordered another when the waitress brought Floyd's coffee.

"Couple of years ago."

"Was it bad? The Years inside?" Floyd wondered how this conversation would go below the surface, but he did not want to push it.

"Actually, no. It could have been a lot worse. But, as you see, I survived."

"I'm glad. What do you do now?"

"Gardening. For the city."

"That's nice," was all she could think of to say. He put the tip of his forefinger gently on the back of her hand and said: "You look well, Mrs. Shaw. Hardly a day older than that day."

"Do we really want to talk about that day?" Penelope's phone started ringing in her handbag.

"Excuse me. I have to get this. I should have been in the office already." She took the call, talked for a few minutes and stood up from her chair.

"Sorry, I have to go. There is a crisis and no one to take care of it." Hesitating, she asked: "Shall I see you again?"

"Only if you want to." She took a business card from her purse and handed it to him.

"Give me a call, will you? Soon."

"Sure." She walked out and Floyd ordered more coffee and breakfast.

* * * *

To get through the day Floyd walked the streets, browsed through the flea-markets, had a late lunch at a street cafe close to the beach and then walked some more. By four o' clock he was tired, went to his hotel-room to rest and refresh and to make a phone call. He dialed the number on the card Penelope gave him. Voicemail. He left a message with his number. Less than half-an-hour later she called back.

"Where can we meet?" He told her where he stayed and she chose a street cafe close by where they can have something to drink. He doubted she would call him, but was carefully excited at the prospect of seeing her. What they were going to talk about, he had no idea. Start all over, take on where they left off, or steer clear of the past and just enjoy the evening? He had nothing planned.

* * * *

They sat down where they could watch passers-by and get a glimpse of the ocean between the buildings. She had white wine, he ordered pineapple juice. He asked about her day, she told him; asked about his day and he told her. Some more chit-chat followed, about the weather, the economy, social media and so on. She asked about prison, he asked about Brendon's business.

"It is no longer his business. I took over everything, made it new. It is now my company."

"I know. I did keep track. I just meant ..."

"You really want to talk about the past, don't you? For the life of me I can't see any reason why. Why would we want to bring up those unhappy times. I have moved on and I have no desire to look back. I have no desire to dig up old dead cows and talk about them. What purpose would it serve? You did time for that day." She looked away, out to the ocean.

"That day everything changed. No talking can change it back, and I don't want to. Neither change it back, nor talk about it ever again."

"There are things that need to be said. Between you and me."

"Like what? I said no. Let's ..."

"I think, maybe we should. Since I did your time for you." Penelope's jaw dropped, all color drained from her face. With big scared eyes she looked at him.

"You have nothing to be scared of. I never regretted taking the fall for you. I'd do it in a flash again if I had to. I meant what I said in court. I loved you. And now I know I still do."

"What do you want from me," she asked in a husky voice.

"I don't really know. I just wanted to see you again. I didn't even plan to tell you that I know."

"But how? How do you know it was ... "

"I saw you. I heard him threatening you, I saw you rushing into the house. When you came back out, you had the gun. He cussed you, called you names, threatened you again and then you pulled the trigger. You heard people moving on the patio and you got scared, I think. Because then you dropped the gun in the bush and walked over to the patio. I picked it up, cleaned off your finger-prints and made sure to leave mine."

"I don't know what to say. All this time I thought no one knew. I could never figure out why you did it. Why you confessed. It was because you knew."

"Yes. I knew and I loved you. I couldn't let you bear the consequences. He hurt you so many times, he deserved it. He got what was coming and I couldn't let them take you away. I couldn't let them punish you, hurt you more than you've already been hurt. I couldn't let them put you through a trial with equal chances of getting acquitted or convicted."

"This is all too much." She stood up, placed a number of Dollar bills on the table and said: "Let's walk." Floyd followed her down to the beach in silence. He did not say a word. Let her break the silence. She had much to think about. Let her think and then the words would come. However long it took her to consume and process it all, he would be there, waiting patiently.

They walked miles before she stopped and turned to him.

"What now from here?"

"I don't know, Penny, I really don't. I cannot expect you to love me. It's not something one person can force on another. You either love me or you don't. If you do, I'll stay, if you don't I'll go and never bother you again."

"What if I can learn to love you, given time?"

"I won't be hanging on a string, Penny. I won't stay around at your convenience."

"That's not what I meant. I mean I've grown fond of you before. Really fond of you. Could this feeling grow deeper?"

"Do you want it to grow deeper?" At this point he knew he would stay even if it were only at her convenience.

"I honestly don't know. Only time can tell. "

* * * *

His parole officer was curious about his trip to New Orleans. Nevertheless he did not contest the application. Floyd's reasons that he was on annual leave from his job and longed for warmer weather, seemed in order. He knew he worked hard and deserved a break. The application to leave the state and have a holiday break at the coast was approved.

Time passed far too slowly for him. He worked harder than before, just so he wouldn't think. In prison he couldn't put her out of his mind. If he did, he might not have made it. Every thought of her helped keeping him from going insane. Now that he was out, now that he saw her again, and with parole almost over, he allowed the occasional thought to linger, but not too long. It is difficult, especially over weekends when he did not work. And at night. The image of her as he last saw her on the beach that night. Her face, her mouth, her eyes full of puzzlement. The wind in her hair. His desire to touch her, to hold her. But the best he allowed himself, was to hold her hand a few short seconds before they said good bye.

But time did pass. On the last day of his parole, he said 'so long' to his parole officer and went straight to his room. He had already given notice. The previous night was his last. This day was a new day. A new life lay ahead.

Bags packed and ready to go, he looked through the room, made sure everything was clean and tidy to his satisfaction. He grabbed his bags, a case on wheels and a shoulder bag was all he needed, locked the door behind him and walked away without looking back. Near the bus station he entered an all-night diner, ordered coffee and a take-away sandwich, got a newspaper and on a stool by the counter, waited for the bus to arrive. He was one of the first to board, chose a seat halfway to the back on the right side of the isle. A window seat. At precisely six fifteen pm the bus started moving, into the traffic, onto the highway going south. Twenty-one hours, fifteen minutes, seven lay overs, thankfully no transfers. All the way down to Atlanta, Georgia.

CHAPTER 7

A Free Man

Maggie was glad to see him. She grabbed him, hugged him and kissed him on both cheeks, then steered him through to the kitchen to feed him. They exchanged news and she did most of the talking. What did he have to say about the past twenty years, after all. It was almost like before, when they sat at the kitchen table in the mansion gossiping about their employers. Only difference now, was they avoided mentioning either Mr. or Mrs. Shaw.

She told him about her daughter and son-in-law who would be home soon, the grandchildren who were both away at college, and life in general. Retired and nowhere to go, her daughter insisted she moved in with them. It was a huge thing for her, adapting to life in Atlanta after living most of her life in New York. But she loved it and did not regret the decision to accept her daughter's offer for a moment.

Then, out of the blue she asked: "What are you going to do about Penny?"

"Question is what is she going to do about me? I saw her while I was still on parole. We talked. Of course she was shocked when I told her."

"You did? What was her reaction?"

"She was scared at first. Thought I came to threaten her, or something. She didn't say much. Didn't know what to say. Of course I reassured her, told her I was not there to harm her in any way. Perhaps the possibility that I might want to blackmail her, crossed her mind."

"And she really never suspected it. Never even considered the possibility of you knowing the truth?"

"According to her reaction, no."

"So, what's next?"

"That was exactly what she asked me. All I can say is that I don't know. I'll go to New Orleans, start a new life and see what happens."

"And if things don't work out for you there, you're welcome to come back here and start over right here in Atlanta. Life is good, peaceful and slow. I'm sure you could find a garden or two to fix. The gardening season here is quite a bit longer than up north."

"Or maybe I can write my memoirs."

"Excellent idea."

"Hi, Mom," a woman said, entering the kitchen, kissing Maggie on the cheek. "You wanna introduce me to your friend?"

"Cindy, this is Floyd Davies. Floyd, my daughter, Cindy."

"Nice meeting you, Mr. Davies. And welcome to Atlanta. Mom, did you show him his room?"

"My goodness, no. We've been talking since he arrived at, what was it? About four ó clock?"

"Are you sure it's no inconvenience for you?"

"Of course not, Mr. Davies, we love to have you."

"Please, call me Floyd."

"OK, Floyd, let me take you through, so you can freshen up before supper."

* * * *

After Floyd spent two nights at Maggie's place, it was time to go. Cindy and her husband, Cliff showed typical southern hospitality and made him feel at home. Though he enjoyed his stay very much, he did not want to impose. It was time to move on. New Orleans was waiting. And perhaps Penelope was waiting too, but he had doubts.

Very early in the morning he thanked Maggie, Cindy and Cliff for their hospitality and for storing his stuff for such a long time. Cliff took good care of his pick-up truck. It was clean and fired up at the first attempt. In the semi-darkness he drove off, waved one last time knowing Maggie was still watching. Maggie waved back as the red tail lights grew smaller and disappeared around a corner. *If only I were ten years younger*, she thought.

The drive down to New Orleans reminded him of his drifter years. The loss of his wife and child drove him on to the next destination, and the next, nowhere to settle again. When he ran out of money, he stayed and did whatever work he could find. With a little money in his pocket, it was time to move on again. Criss-crossing North-America he later moved on over the border to Mexico, Guatemala, Honduras, Nicaragua, further on through Costa Rica and Panama, then into Columbia where he spent more time to work and earn money again. Then on through Brazil.

He spent over a year in Brazil before he went further south to Argentine. In Bahía Blanca he sold his pick-up, got a job on a cargo ship headed for Sri Lanka, but got off as soon as they docked in at the harbor in Table Bay. Climbing Table Mountain was a challenge, but once on top, the spectacular view was enough reward. As he sat there, watching the sun setting over the Atlantic Ocean, his thoughts drifted back over all the wonders of nature he had seen and experienced. The subtle color changes and the depths of the Grand Canyon, the forests and swamps of Florida, the watery planes of the Amazon and the Pantanal with their hundreds of colored birds flying over the waterways. Competing in beauty, it was difficult to choose one place over the other. Each had its own special character, ambiance.

He backpacked through the country of South-Africa, saw many more interesting places, like the Winelands of the Boland, the Karroo where the air was as fresh as on the prairie near his hometown and the stars at night as bright as in Texas. In the folds of the Swartberg mountain range, he found a place called The Hell because of its heat and inaccesebility, and because of the remoteness from the rest of the world, the people were the friendliest, most hospitable he had encountered, only too happy to get to talk to someone from the outside. In spite of their isolation, they were not backward or ignorant. From there he turned south-east again toward the ocean through the Tsitsikama forest to Knysna.

Deadly Innocent

He saw many more places, from the salt plains in Namibia, to the Big Hole near Kimberley, game in the Addo Elephant Park, kosmos flowers in the Free State, the majestic Drakensberg Mountains in Natal, and reached Johannesburg in late October when the city was clothed in purple. From any high point, the Jacaranda trees, in full bloom, cast a pale purple haze as far as the eye could reach. Many streets were covered under a purple canopy that casted a purple carpet underneath. But careful, walking under the trees might be hazardous. The freshly fallen blossoms make a clapping sound as they get stepped on, but they become a slippery mess as foot traffic increases. In contrast, looking east from Brixton late in the afternoon, the sun reflected gold from every window in midtown Johannesburg. The city of gold.

The first thing that happened to him setting foot in Johannesburg, was getting mugged. He went to Pretoria, got hit over the head and robbed in bright daylight. He was picked up on the sidewalk after lying there, bleeding for half an hour before someone realized he was not a drunken bum, but needed help. It was a man in his late middle ages who helped him up, took him to a hospital and offered to pay his bill. He was kept overnight for observation.

Early the next morning, as soon as he was discharged, his well-doer, Pieter Nel, he said his name was, met him and took him to a coffee shop to buy him a proper breakfast. Pieter Nel was a businessman who just popped out of the office to get a bite to eat, when he saw Floyd lying there and took pity on him. Floyd told him his story, Pieter offered to help him find a job and recommended a boardinghouse where he could find affordable accommodation. When, after a week Floyd could find no job, he decided to move on. He said goodbye to Pieter, promised to stay in touch, and headed north, then east, on toward the lovely town of Nelspruit. In Waterfal-Boven, he stayed a few days, but employment was rare in those areas.

Back in Johannesburg he found temporary employment and accommodation at the YMCA in Braamfontein. It did not take long to learn how to take care of himself so he would not get mugged again. Unlike New York where you often had to walk wherever you needed to go, in Johannesburg you take a bus or taxi to avoid getting jumped. Thinking back, his time in Johannesburg was not bad. He made a few good friends, some of whom were still in contact with him.

* * * *

Closing in on Mobile, Floyd opened the window to smell the sea air. He passed Mobile and made a stop at Biloxi to stretch his legs and have a bite to eat. He ordered a pancake with syrup and cream and a tall coffee. Walking around some more after the snack, stretching, he was now ready for the last shift of the journey into the sunset. The sun was low, almost touching the horizon as he drove over the bridge into the city of New Orleans.

* * * *

Booked into a hotel, having unpacked what he would need for a day of two, he headed out in search of a good meal. Many restaurants offer mainly seafood with little choice of anything else, but he needed a hearty steak or a spicy mutton dish. A couple of blocks away from his hotel he found what he wanted. For the first time in many years, he ordered a glass of red wine. If wine were on the prison menu, he did not know about it. They never showed him a menu, he thought with a smirk.

Satisfied after the wine, a lamb stew, and two cups of coffee, he was ready to take a long walk before turning in. He walked for an hour, thinking of Penelope only. Where was she at the moment? What was she doing right now? He would not contact her before he was settled in. First get himself organized, then let her know he was there. And what would her reaction be? She was in shock the last time they saw each other. Her reaction and words should not be taken seriously. He was so much older that her. She could have any man she wanted. But what if she was really ready and willing to give him a chance? He, a gardener, she a business tycoon? The thought is so laughable, it almost made him cringe and run back all the way to New York.

His heart raced at the thought that she might want him, yet he was careful not to get his hopes up. At a street cafe, he ordered coffee, sipped it slowly and walked at an easy pace back to his hotel. With winter approaching, the nights were cool. After a shower, Floyd slipped into a light sweat suit and fell asleep quickly. Around midnight he woke up after a strange dream: Penelope made coffee, poured it into a flask, with her back turned to him, she emptied a small packet of powder of some sort into the coffee, shook it lightly and handed it to him.

He went to the bathroom, drank a pint of water and went back to sleep, just to wake up two hours later after another dream: He carried the flask with coffee to his car. Penelope followed with a picnic basket and they drove off to the Grand Canyon. Instead of a festive mood, there was something sinister in the atmosphere between them. He sat up, rubbed his eyes and went for another drink of water. Fatigue made him fall asleep again.

The dream was now like a sequel: He stood behind Penelope on the edge of a high spot looking out over the canyon. Suddenly she started sliding, faster and faster down the cliff. In slow motion she stretched out her hands towards him, but he just stood there, staring at her as she went down into the depth. He heard her body hitting one rock after the other on her way to the bottom. An avalanche of rocks and gravel followed her and then, silence. He unscrewed the top of the flask and woke up just as he was about to take a gulp of the poisoned coffee. Exhausted he fell asleep again. When he woke up hours later, he could not remember whether he pushed her off the cliff, or whether she slipped on the loose gravel.

* * * *

Freedom. What it meant to him, was that he was free to come and go as he pleased; free to settle in New Orleans or stay a while and move on. It was his decision. His decision depended partially on Penelope; what she wanted or did not want; what she expected of him and was willing to give him. He wanted more, but friendship would be enough.

He scrambled these thoughts around in his mind while walking the streets to get to know the city. Last night's dream, however, kept coming back to him. He did not believe the notion that dreams meant anything, or could predict the future. Yet, he could not shake off the ominous feeling it left inside his spirit. Perhaps it was a mistake to break contact after he came to see her while he was on parole. If they were communicating, he would have known what was happening in her life. He would have had a better idea what to expect. Following her through the media and even social media provided some sort of barometer, but it was not reliable on a personal level.

Stalking is an ugly word. Observation sounds better. That was what he would do. He would observe her movements, her life style for a few days; then he'd give her a call to get together for a drink.

A week passed in which he learned much about her routine, friends, business associates and her social hangouts. He learned that she lived a relatively quiet life. Her company kept her too busy to live a very active social life. She often accepted invitations to business dinners and parties, sometimes alone, sometimes accompanied by one of two, of her seven male business partners, two were single. Sometimes there was this man from her past, a "family friend" of the Shaw family. Greg Atwood. Floyd saw him on the night of the murder. He was the one waiting for Brendon outside just before Penelope shot him. His presence in New Orleans was somewhat disturbing.

* * * *

They met for coffee at least twice a week, had dinner once a week and chatted as if the years in between, had not happened. Slowly and cautiously their friendship grew to a higher level. She began to share confidential issues about her business and her personal life with him, tapped from his wisdom in many situations and brightened his day with her joys. Together they laughed, sighed and marveled at life in general. They spent times casually together that included arm-in-arm walks through town and on the beach, sitting on park benches, enjoying meals and coffees at restaurants with a view.

Penelope invited him to a small thanksgiving party. Only a few friends attended, singles who lived far away from any close relatives. He gave her a small Christmas gift for which she thanked him with a tight hug and a two-second kiss on the lips. Floyd wanted to take her out on a formal date on New Year's Eve. She cancelled at the last minute saying something about a surprise visit from her sister who lived in Canada. He knew about the sister, but had never met her.

After New Year, Penelope's working pace picked up, sometimes she seemed withdrawn and they saw less of each other. He thought it might be his imagination, but he couldn't shake the feeling that something was bothering her. Nevertheless, their times together seemed to grow steadily closer. She told him things about herself that she had never told anyone else. Personal things she never spoke about. Like the baby she lost twenty-five weeks before it should have been born. Like life in general with Brendon, the career in education she never pursued, her second marriage to a lazy womanizer who was never satisfied with one woman at a time, and her personal likes and dislikes.

She asked him about his life, but he always changed the subject. When insisting he told her something about himself, he finally told her about Angie and his son, his world travels, all the time giving as little detail as possible, and emotionally detached as if he was giving an account of daily business. They walked, talked and laughed together, getting to know each other better and better.

They were sitting on a bench overlooking the ocean when Penelope suddenly grew serious, looked intently at him and said: "We never talk about Brendon anymore."

"Why should we? Hasn't everything been said already?"

"There are things I have never discussed with anyone. It's a burden I no longer want to carry alone. Floyd, you are the only person I can tell everything. You know me better than anybody on this Earth."

"If you really want to, need to talk, I'm listening."

"That night. Brendon met someone. He came to see him and together they walked outside. The man was a spy, an informant. He sold information of his company to rival companies. He was not in favor of his company taking over Brendon's because it would compromise his own position. He gathered information and brought it to Brendon to be used the very next day to stop the take-over"

"But shouldn't that have been good news for Brendon? Why was he so upset when the man left?"

"Brendon asked him for a specific document, but he could not lay his hands on it."

"And then you appeared on the scene."

"Yes. I was looking for Brendon to tell him his brother had left and said goodbye. He got more upset when he realized I saw him with Williams."

"Why would that upset him? Everyone else saw him with Williams."

"A few weeks before, I overheard one of his partners talking to him about Williams. He warned Brendon against him, saying he is a scoundrel whose word is not reliable. Brendon promised not to have any dealings with him again. He accused me of eavesdropping. That night I went to bed with a black eye."

"And then you came out, saw him and he thought you were eavesdropping again?"

"Something like that, yes. He threatened me with a severe beating as soon as the party was over."

"Then you went inside and found a gun. Where did you find it? Did you know the combination to the save?" She dropped her eyes, studied her shoes.

"Yes. There were two guns in the safe. I took one, loaded it and rushed outside before anyone could catch me in his study." She looked far out over the ocean.

"I was not prepared to take another beating."

"What did you do after that?"

"I went inside, to the ladies room and washed my hands. Over and over, I washed them until someone came in and I had to finish and go back to the party. I drank a glass of wine as fast as I could to stop my hands from shaking. I tried to act normal, but there is no way of knowing whether I fooled everyone. Until they told me you have been arrested. I could faint at that moment."

"Why?"

"Surprise, disbelief, relief in a way, I guess. I was expecting to be arrested."

"And then the trial. You were very convincing. Were you scared that I would be acquitted and that they will look at you again as a suspect?"

"I was in such a daze, I hardly thought about it. Just went through the motions. Like a robot, got up every morning hoping you would be found innocent, but not ponder on it much. Why did you do it, Floyd? Why did you take the fall for me?"

"Jesus paid my fines and did so with his blood. I loved you, that was the least I could do for you."

"Do you really believe all that's in the Bible?"

"I believe it, all, and I live by it, or try to."

"Wish I could believe in anything so strongly that I'd be willing to make such a sacrifice." She rubbed her arms: "It's getting chilly. I think we should go." He stood, took her hand and together they walked towards a cafe close by and ordered coffee.

CHAPTER 8

The Wedding

Late spring in New Orleans. It was a small but expensive wedding with only a few carefully selected guests. The front garden of the newly acquired mansion was the perfect venue for the reception. Beautifully decorated with flowers and ribbons everywhere; a hundred candles to be lit soon; soft classical music in the background and the best caterers in town, the wedding planner made sure it would be a day to remember for the happy couple as well as the small number of wealthy guests, who were used to the best.

Floyd did not accept the invitation. Sitting in his truck parked near the chapel, he saw the bride as she came out and was helped into the car by her new husband. Why, he thought, do some women choose the wrong man every time? Why don't they learn? Long after they had left for the reception he sent the nose of his truck in an easterly direction towards Florida. At an all-night diner just outside Fort Walton Beach he pulled in for fuel and coffee. One cup down and one on the go, he hit the road again and did not stop before the night sky started coloring in the east.

Lake City seemed a good place to stop for breakfast. He spent almost an hour eating slowly and then stretching his legs before he resumed his journey to who knows where. The sun was up by the time he reached Jacksonville.

I'm not a drifter anymore, Floyd told himself. Too old to go travel the world, no taste for it anymore. And he liked this city. It was no longer for Penelope's sake he wanted to stay. There are many other cities where he could have gone to settle, but he grew to like New Orleans. It is a place with ambiance. And he liked the climate. He just needed a break.

After driving miles around in Florida, south form Jacksonville through Daytona Beach, Ford Lauderdale, Miami, he then took the highway over the Florida Keys. What an exceptional experience. Floyd did not care much for the animal interactive programs, but immensely enjoyed the parrot shows. Farther on down the road the smells, and the views of the sea in all the different shades, tints and mixes of blues, greens, purples and turquois, the keys with their lush sub-tropical vegetation, all of it provided balm for his aching heart and weary soul.

He drove right up to Key West with a most spectacular sunset in front of him. The next day he walked barefoot on the sugar-white sand, sat on a rock, watching the clear water at his feet, stopped by the most southern point and stared out over the ocean as if he could see Cuba, ninety miles away to the south. He had a fish sandwich and a beer at the Tiki Bar, Creekside Restaurant then almost in a hurry, took to the road, heading home to New Orleans. Enough traveling. Time to settle.

* * * *

Penelope stared out of the window, watching the patchwork-landscape slowly passing by more than thirty-thousand feet below. On her way to her third honeymoon. Was this the right thing? Is Greg Atwood the right man for her? David loved her. Now that he was single, wouldn't he be a better choice? He was very likeable, but she did not love him, she was thinking. Simon always had a soft spot for her, but he is happily married and she hadn't seen much of him and Tilda since Brendon's death. Funny thing that she was thinking only of the two men in New York whom she knew had a soft spot for her, at this point in her life, having just married a third friend from New York.

And then there is Floyd, she thought. He probably loved her more than anyone alive. She knew she broke his heart. Is that why she kept doubting her choice? Or is there some truth in what Floyd said when she told him she was going to marry Greg? Is Greg only after her money? She turned her head away from the window to look at Greg. Champagne glass in one hand, he touched her arm with his left hand and smiled.

"Love you, Honey. We're on our way to a great life together." Penelope nodded, took a sip of wine and leaned back. Yes, life is going to be great. Greg was by far the most exciting man she had met in a while. Funny that he pitched up at this point in time. Not even her female friends ever visited her in New Orleans. They only expected to see her whenever she was in New York.

He is taking her to Dubai, a place no one else would consider taking her. David would have taken her to Paris, a city she had seen many times. Simon, if he were free, who knows? Tokyo maybe? No thanks. The Far-East never had any attraction for her. Floyd? Cape Town? That would have been nice, but not as exciting as the Middle-East. Yeah, life is going to be good.

* * * *

Back at home after the honeymoon the happy couple lived a very busy social life. One party followed another. For every party they had at the mansion, they were invited to at least two others at friends' houses. Greg was set on showing off his beautiful bride. And beautiful she still was. She carried her years exceptionally well. Greg was known for having a good eye for a woman. He had had enough practice, divorced four times, having gone through girlfriends like most men went through a packet of cigarettes.

When Penelope complained about her need to go to the office and run her company, Greg just laughed and told her to loosen up a bit. Relax and have fun for a change. The company will be there the next day, and the next.

And the next day Greg went with Penelope to the office. Like a good husband, he showed intense interest in everything she did. He wanted to learn about her business to support her better, he told her. She felt flattered, but also a bit irritated when he followed her like a puppy. Whenever he did not follow her, he befriended her staff members.

So it went on for days.

"Greg, I really appreciate your interest in my company, but honey, what about your own business? Don't they need you there?"

"Actually I trust my people to run everything smoothly. They all know what to do. No need for me to hang around there and watch them. When they need me, they'll call."

"Don't you have any other interests? I can't imagine you not eventually getting bored following me all the time."

"I love following you. Besides, when will I get to see my wife if you're at the office all day and I someplace else?"

"C'mon, it's not that bad. We spend a lot of time together. I have breakfast at home and I leave the office to have dinner with you every night. I do not work weekends. So, why don't you take up golf, or some hobby?"

"Do I get the impression you don't want me at the office? Why's that, why would you not want me at the office?"

"You know that's not true. I love your companionship. But I have to work and you distract me, know what I mean?" She smiled sweetly at him and blew a kiss over the table.

"Now if you put it that way. But would it bother you if I tag along just once in a while?"

"Not at all. Just as long as you don't chat up the office girls."

"There is only one girl I like to chat up, the one I already own." She considered it a strange thing to say, but instead of commenting, she blew another kiss, took her wine and got up from the table to go to the big family room next to the family dining room. Seating herself into the soft cushions of the deep couch, she switched on the TV and flipped to a news channel to find out what had been happening in the world that day. Greg poured himself a brandy and goblet in one hand, bowl of chocolate and nuts in the other he joined her on the couch.

* * * *

Back home, Floyd considered his future. He had to have something to focus on. Physically still strong and energetic, it would be a waste to settle in retirement and wait for death to release him. He had too much life still in him, a life that had to be lived. Lord, Jesus, show me the way. It is not yet time to give up

But what can I do to keep busy? Have to have something to get up in the morning for, he thought, walking the streets as usual. He knew every street in New Orleans by now. Or most of them, anyway. He knew every coffee shop, every diner, every bistro, most restaurants; he ate at most of them, never twice in one place. He browsed the flea markets, spoke to people to find out what was trendy, what was out and what demand was in short supply. That way he got to know more than just the city streets, but the people that made the city what it was.

* * * *

Every city had gardens. Every garden needed to be taken care of. And to take care of a garden, tools and supplies were needed. New Orleans did not have enough supply shops. Floyd had little trouble setting up a small supply shop in a small shopping center in the heart of a middle class suburb, Palm Hill, where many people tended their own gardens.

Professional gardening services and landscapers also needed supplies. Floyd connected with a few and offered supplies at discount prices if required in large quantities.

Students in need of casual work were in ample supply in a city that had a big university. Floyd appointed a student part time to help in the shop and do deliveries. By the end of the following summer, his little venture had become well known, started showing a nice profit and provided enough distraction from the source of his broken heart.

Life turned out to be good. He was free, he was busy and he was happy, well sort of. In his tiny apartment above the shop, he lived his life independently, the way he liked it. Simple furniture and decor proved a simple life style for a man who did not need every comfort and luxury available. Early up and on the go, he did not have the energy at night to roam the streets or lie awake staring at the ceiling. After a hard day at work, he used to prepare a quick meal or get a take-out, which he ate in front of the TV where he often fell asleep.

* * * *

Greg carried on visiting Penelope's office, mostly unannounced. When he was home alone, he went through her personal documents and learned things that he should not consider himself with. He needed to know everything there was to know about her company. He'll show those big shots in New York a thing or two. Blaming him for not being able to frame Williams for Brendon's murder! Imagine. What was he supposed to do? Everything was going well until this gardener character stepped in and killed the man that was supposed to be killed by Greg himself so he could put the blame on Williams, and rid the company of that two-faced traitor. So they were stuck with Williams and let him, Greg go. He'll do his own take-over and show them. It was more than luck, it was fate that made him bump into Penelope at the party.

Greg kept on fiddling around in Penelope's drawers and cabinets so see what he could find that was valuable. Information that might help him to accomplish his mission. He did find a few documents that might be helpful. For instance the little address book he found in a drawer of her home-office desk. There were all kinds of coded entries. Some looked like passwords. Some looked like account details. Now is this my lucky day or what, he thought. There was also one entry that particularly interested him. Floyd Davies and a cell number. The name rang a bell and he did a little research. He dialed the number.

"Palm Hill Garden Supplies, Floyd speaking." Greg put the phone down. So that's where mister gardener is hanging out these days. But what on earth is he doing in New Orleans? Of all the places he could go to, he chose this city? Could it be that he is after Penelope? And she obviously knew he was there. He wondered if they were still in contact. How convenient, he thought. How absolutely convenient. His plan is falling into place. There were several options, none of which he was completely comfortable with. But now things started to look very interesting. With these new possibilities, his plan just became a whole lot clearer. A whole lot more viable.

CHAPTER 9

Another Murder

The phone rang. Of course it was after hours, so no one answered. The next morning Floyd checked his messages and wrote the number down that was given by the voice on the answering service. He dialed the number. No answer. He left a message. The next morning there was a message from the same number. He called again, no answer. Later he tried again, still no answer. He decided to wait till closing time and then try again.

During the afternoon he got busy with a number of orders that had to be delivered, and forgot to call. He went out for a bite at a deli close by and when he passed his shop on his way up to his apartment, he remembered about the call. In no mood to unlock his shop at this hour, he decided against his mood and went in to make the call. Again no answer.

Thoroughly fed-up, he decided to ignore that number and delete it every time it might be repeated in future. While he was in the shower, his cell phone rang. Being tired and ready to fall asleep, he ignored that missed call and went straight to bed. A shock wave went through him the next morning when he checked his cell phone and saw the missed call was from Penelope.

Greg woke her very early handing her her cell phone.

"Early call for you, Honey," he said.

"Floyd! Hi," she looked at Greg, horrified to be hearing Floyd's voice after so many months.

"I got a please-call-me from you last night. Sorry I didn't call right back. Is everything OK?"

"You did? But I didn't sent you one. How?"

"There was a missed call also. And then the pcm. Are you sure?"

"Sure I'm sure."

"So, you're OK?"

"Yeah. I'm OK. You?"

"I'm fine, thanks. Sorry for the misunderstanding."

"It's OK." She glanced at Greg again, feeling guilty for not having Floyd's number deleted from her contact list.

"All right, bye, then."

"Take care, Floyd. Bye." Yawning, Greg asked her what that was all about.

"A very funny thing. I thought my phone was off, but this person said he got a pcm from me last night."

"Strange, yes. But maybe your phone fell, or something, which turned his name on. Don't worry about it. Is that all he said?"

"Well, yes, of course he asked if I'm well, just to be polite, I guess."

"Who is he. You called him Floyd? It sounds familiar."

"Just someone I know. Knew. Haven't had contact in a while."

"Well, since his name is still on your contact list, he must have been a good friend. And he sounds concerned about you. Why don't you invite him over? He can join us for cocktails on Friday night."

"No, I don't think it's a good idea. We were not that close. Just leave it be."

"Come on, Penny, I insist. Invite the guy. If he's single we can always hook him up with Mavis. She'll be here and always ready for a new romance."

"He's too old for Mavis. He must be approaching his seventies already."

"If he's nice, Mavis won't mind. Come on. Call him right now."

"I said no. And that's final. Look, I'm wide awake now. I'll get into the shower and go to the office early." With that, she hopped out of bed and walked briskly to her bathroom. Greg made sure she was covered in lather before he picked up her cell phone and send a text to Floyd inviting him to the party, telling him: 'my husband insists' and giving the address and the time thirty minutes earlier than the expected arrival time of the other guests.

The reply came immediately: Are you sure? I don't think it's a good idea. To which Greg quickly replied: I told you my husband wants to meet you. Please, just this once.

OK, I'll be there, but I won't stay long.

Thnx a mil. U won't regret it. The shower taps were turned off. Greg had to work fast. He switched the phone off, fiddled with the battery so that it won't switch on again. He had to make sure there was no further communication between the two. When she came out of the bathroom, the phone was lying on her night stand and Greg was laying with his back turned to her, pretending to be asleep.

* * * *

Floyd parked his truck in front of the big house and knocked on the door. Having made sure no servants were around, Greg opened the door and invited him in.

"Hi, I'm Greg Atwood," he said, "welcome," offering his hand. Floyd shook it reluctantly introducing himself. He was hoping Penelope would greet him at the door, or a butler, or anyone else but Greg.

"Floyd Davies? Name sounds familiar. Oh, yes, Penelope mentioned she wanted to invite you, but wasn't sure you'd come. So I insisted she invite you. Glad you could make it, Floyd." They were still standing in the entrance hall. Somewhere to the left loud music could be heard.

"Just a moment. I'll show you to the reception room in a sec. Honey," he yelled in the direction of the stair case. "Come on down now. The guests are arriving." He turned to talk to Floyd, facing the staircase, so that Floyd would be facing away from the staircase.

"So, you are the brave guy who killed Brendon Shaw. I was ready to do that, but you got to him first. You have no idea how inconvenient that was. And you have no idea how convenient your presence is tonight."

"What do you mean?"

"Once a murderer, always a murderer. You are going to kill again tonight. You said in court you loved her. Perhaps you still do. They say a woman scorned is bad, but just watch what a scorned man can do. You are a scorned man, aren't you?" Greg's lips twisted mockingly. They heard footsteps on the staircase. Penelope was coming down. Floyd looked up, when he turned back, Greg was holding a pistol. Realizing what he intended, Floyd opened his mouth to yell at Penelope, who had almost reached the foot of the staircase. She was in shock when she recognized Floyd, and then she saw the pistol in Greg's hand. Unbelieving what was before her, uncomprehending what was happening, she leapt forward, the last move she made in this life. The pistol fired, Penelope fell at the foot of the staircase, blood pouring out of her chest. Then a second shot followed, Greg screamed when blood started oozing from a wound in his left shoulder.

* * * *

The tape was playing over and over in his mind, and in slow motion. In reality it played out in seconds. He still could not believe what had just happened. He had wanted to scream, to yell at her, tell her not to come down, to go back up the stairs: "No! don't …" but it was too late. Before he could utter a sound, she was laying on the floor, a pool of blood spreading from under her over the floor, his ears still ringing from the clap of the gunshots. And now the gun was pointing at him, aimed at his heart. Jesus, Jesus, help me.

"You will do exactly as I tell you," said Greg, motioning with the gun. "You will get into your car and drive away as fast as you can."

"Why? What about ... her? What about the police? What ...?"

"Shut up and go. Now. Or I'll shoot you and tell the police you shot her and then yourself. Now I'm giving you a fair chance to get away and forget what just happened." Greg lifted the gun higher and aimed at Floyd's head, snarling: "go now."

How he managed to reach his truck, fire it up, put it in gear and drive away he would never know. How he managed to evade the approaching police, he had no idea. But he was not about to leave without finding out what was happening at the mansion. Before the first patrol car arrived, he disappeared round the first corner, turned right at the next intersection and parked behind a wall near the entrance to the closest big house.

Trying to control the shaking in his hands, he worked fast to retrieve an overhaul, a tool and a cover for the truck. He quickly put on the overhaul over his clothes, put the secateurs, the first tool he could grab, in his overhaul pocket, put a cap on his head, pulled the weather-cover over the truck and casually strolled round the corner to the house, where there were now several police cars, an ambulance and a number of bystanders, would-be guests at the Atwood cocktail party.

Slowly, clipping his way along the shrubs on the sidewalk, he moved closer to the scene. Keeping open his ears, he tried to hear what people were saying. After a short while one of the police cars dashed out of the driveway radioing ahead to alert other cars in the vicinity to look out for who knows what. Then he heard one bystander say to another: "They are looking for a truck. The driver apparently shot someone and got away before the police arrived."

"Who got shot?"

"I think it's the woman. Mr. Atwood's wife."

"Look, they're bringing out the body. Hey, man," he looked straight at Floyd and said: "It's Friday, it's late, sun's going down already. Do you always work this late?" Another laughed and said: "I wish my gardener was so diligent. Fridays he puts down tools at noon." Yet another said: "He's probably curious, hanging around to find out what's going on."

"Go on, you, take a hike. Show's over. You can go home and tell your wife all the excitement."

"Or your buddies at the bar." So they kept on mocking him. Humbly he turned and left, walking in the opposite direction of where his car was. So, they're looking for my truck, probably as described by Greg. The man really did his home-work and planned it all out well, he thought. The police were probably already waiting at his apartment. If he drove home, they would probably chase him down and shoot him on site. That's probably what Greg Atwood was counting on, Floyd thought.

Considering various options on what his next move should be, he made a decision. There was no escaping; they will find him. Best is to go find them. He walked more than a mile before finding the first gas station. In the rest room he removed his cap and overhaul and called a cab.

"Nearest police station," he told the driver. Inside the station he worked his way to the top, insisting on talking to the officer in charge, concerning a murder investigation. He sat himself down in front of the big man's desk and started talking.

"A murder has been committed and I want to make a statement."

"Did you commit the murder?"

"No, I'm a witness."

"Tell me what you saw." Floyd told the whole story from the first phone call to his shop to the moment he walked into the police station. He left out a few things, like stalking the murder scene in his gardening overhaul, and exactly where his truck was

"Why would he choose you? Is there a reason why he considered you to be a suitable choice as someone to frame for this murder?"

"Because I was once in love with his wife. And because I was convicted of murder twenty-six years ago." He told the whole story of Brendon's death, the court case and what followed.

"What do you consider to be Greg Atwood's motive for murdering his wife. You say they were married only about five months?"

"Money, greed, incompetence to make it big on his own. Mrs. Atwood was a wealthy woman."

"I'm sure Mr. Atwood's version of the events will differ greatly from your own. Why should I believe your story?"

"I'm telling the truth. He won't be. He'll insist on making me look guilty."

"Do you have anything concrete? Any proof of your innocence?"

"No. But maybe forensics can help. I want you to get them here now."

"What can they do to help you?"

"If I shot anyone, there should be residue on my hands and clothes. There won't be found any. But I'm sure Mr. Atwood's hands and clothes will not be clean. He might still be at the emergency to get his wound stitched. The wound in his shoulder where he shot himself so he could say I tried to kill them both. Also, my fingerprints won't be found on the gun."

* * * *

According to the newspapers the next morning, Greg's version of the events of the previous night was indeed different from his. In his statement he said that Floyd had made several phone calls to the house, but said nothing. The records can be checked. When no one called him back, he called Penelope's cell phone. She sounded upset when she talked to him, but she wouldn't tell what he had said to her. He, Greg, then got upset and confronted her. There was an argument which made her cave in and tell the truth.

She told him they had planned on leaving together, but she was having second thoughts. Large amounts of money had already been transferred from her accounts to various other accounts, so that they can live in luxury some place and not worry about her company, which she would have left in his, Greg's hands. The fact that the money transfers were done by Greg himself, was, of course never mentioned.

According to Greg, they were lovers while Brendon was still alive. The moment he was released from prison, they resumed their affair. Greg only found out about it that morning when she told him. He pleaded with her not to leave him and she told him she had already changed her mind. She was not in love with Floyd anymore, but didn't know how to tell him, because he had such an explosive temperament. She was afraid. The next afternoon, Friday, while they were expecting guests for a cocktail, he stormed into the house and threatened him, Greg. Penelope appeared on the scene, told Floyd to leave her alone and that was when he pulled out a gun and started shooting. He wounded him in the shoulder but Penelope was killed, probably instantly.

There was nothing in the papers about Floyd's statement. Neither was there anything about Greg already being in custody for the murder of Penelope Atwood.

After the forensic detectives tested Floyd's hands, took his coat to the lab to be tested, an officer drove him to where he left his truck. Retrieving the vehicle, he drove home, still in shock to think she was gone. His Penelope, his great love after so many years of mourning Angie and his son.

Greg was convicted and sentenced to death. A reporter of the New Orleans Post interviewed Floyd, asking him about the case and also the Shaw case.

"Why did you do it?"

"Do what? Shoot Brendon?"

"No, why did you take the wrap for Penelope Shaw? You didn't kill Brendon Shaw. She did, didn't she? Did you really love her that much?"

"I don't know what you're talking about. She was an abused woman. I had to listen how he beat her up more than once. She always had bruises on her arms and neck. Probably everywhere on her body." In his thoughts he said: 'I'm guilty as hell, of many things. Jesus not only did my time, he was willingly executed in my place, because he loved me'.

"You never saw bruises anywhere else?"

"How could I see bruises covered by clothes?"

"Just asking. So, you were not lovers. Just friends. You loved her, but she did not love you back."

Floyd sighed. "That's right. She was fond of me. Said so too. But she never loved me."

"And it didn't make you angry, the fact that she didn't love you?"

"Sad. Not angry. It made me sad."

"Why did you come to New Orleans? Did you mean to pursue her? Get her to love you?"

"I was hoping, of course, but doubtful. Friendship would have been enough though."

"And you did become friends? You're much older than what she was. What made you think she might be romantically interested in you?"

"Have you seen the dog face that prince up north cheated with on his lovely wife? Considering that, anything is possible. As I said, I was hoping, but doubtful. What gave you the idea that I did not kill Brendon Shaw?"

"The case had always bothered me. I was a young journalist in New York in those days. Too many things did not make sense. Like how did the murder weapon got into your possession. I guess you won't tell me. But the police never bothered to investigate. They had their man. End of story."

Floyd's story was told, but nothing was mentioned about the Shaw case. He made the reporter promise he would not bring it up and create the possibility of tarnishing the memory of Penelope. She was no longer there to defend herself.

Deadly Innocent

Twice an innocent man. His innocence proved deadly to three others. Greg Atwood will die in prison. He was getting what he deserved. If Penny did not come rushing out, gun in hand, Greg would have done it. He was not hiding behind the shrubs for nothing. He hated Brendon. He was jealous of him. Everyone knew that. He was waiting for a chance to get to Brendon and was probably shocked to hear a gunshot, maybe seeing him fall, but not the shooter. Shocked to learn someone else had the same idea. Someone else got Brendon first. If he had seen Penny, he would somehow have brought attention to it, or blackmail her. He was a real idiot and stupid as an ass.

Pondering these things, Floyd asked himself why he did not warn Penny. Why was he so self-centered, wallowing in self-pity instead of telling her everything. He could have saved her. Just like in his dream, he saw her falling and did nothing. These thoughts, together with an aching loneliness and longing for Penelope, stabbed right through his heart at every simple reminder of her.

Floyd Davies ran his little gardening supply store for eight more years, sold the business and retired comfortably in a retirement village in the North-Eastern part of town, on a hill overlooking the river in the distance.

www.ingramcontent.com/pod-product-compliance
Lightning Source LLC
Chambersburg PA
CBHW060847050426
42453CB00008B/877